Global Governance

Rechtspolitisches Symposium
Legal Policy Symposium

Herausgegeben im Institut für Rechtspolitik an der Universität Trier
von Bernd von Hoffmann und Gerhard Robbers

Band 2

PETER LANG
Frankfurt am Main · Berlin · Bern · Bruxelles · New York · Oxford · Wien

Bernd von Hoffmann (ed.)

Global Governance

Reports and Discussions of a Symposium held in Trier
on October 9th and 10th, 2003

PETER LANG
Europäischer Verlag der Wissenschaften

Bibliographic Information published by Die Deutsche Bibliothek
Die Deutsche Bibliothek lists this publication in the Deutsche Nationalbibliografie; detailed bibliographic data is available in the internet at <http://dnb.ddb.de>.

ISSN 1610-8906
ISBN 3-631-52770-5
US-ISBN 0-8204-7325-1

www.peterlang.de

TABLE OF CONTENTS

PREFACE 7

I. MULTILATERALISM AND UNILATERALISM AFTER THE IRAQ CONFLICT 9

Meinhard Schröder
The Status of Public International Law Seen from a European Perspective 11

Michael J. Glennon
The UN's Irrelevant Relevance 23

Hanns W. Maull
Globalisation, Politics and the State 31

Discussion 45

II. ACTORS OF GLOBALISATION 55

Klaus Dicke
The United Nations as an Actor of Globalization 57

Discussion 67

Peter Eigen
The Role of NGOs in Global Governance: Controlling Corruption – The Example of Transparency International 71

Discussion 77

Angelika Pohlenz
International Business Needs International Rules 81

Discussion 95

III. GLOBAL DEVELOPMENT POLICY 99

Wolfgang Weiß
The Role of the WTO in Global Development Policy 101

Discussion 131

Olivier Frémond
Findings from the World Bank Corporate Governance Country Assessments 135

El-Shagi El-Shagi
Is Globalisation Detrimental for Developing Countries? 177

Discussion 189

Bernd von Hoffmann
Conclusions 193

LIST OF PARTICIPANTS 197

PREFACE

The Institute for Legal Policy at the University of Trier devotes its second workshop to Global Governance. This relatively new topic is connected namely to economics, political and social science and law. It cannot be treated adequately by one discipline only and by nationals from one country only. Also the experience of practice and the systematic spirit of research as well as the imagination of both are required. The actual composition of this workshop is interdisciplinary and international and it combines theory and practice. Moreover it represents different generations. This is an outstanding forum.

The focus of this workshop is on the actual stage of international relations as well as on future developments. The issue of standards of good global governance will necessarily arise and will be answered controversially. We have at least three issues which will give rise to controversial debate in this workshop:

- the conditions for the use of military power
- the role of the United Nations
- the distribution of wealth between the North and the South.

All these issues are at the top of the global policy agenda. The Institute believes that an open debate is a way to promote new insights for the future.

Before the workshop started, all participants had the abstracts and the papers in their hands. The main purpose of the workshop was the discussion of those papers. Reports on those discussions are part of this volume. A general discussion at the end of the workshop identified the central issues. The conclusions which form part of this volume are based on that general discussion; they are – however – in the sole responsibility of the editor. The cooperation of all contributors in editing their papers is gratefully acknowledged.

A special word of thanks goes to Julia Stunz who took an essential part in the organisation of the workshop and the editing of the book. Invaluable assistance was also given by the Trier law students Christiane Bill, André Eichhofer, Sören Havenith, Anna B. Koch, Hauke Kuder and Anna Radjuk. They prepared protocols of the discussions under the coordination of Malte Beyer. The Institute's staff gave support to the workshop and Claudia Lehnen prepared the manuscripts for the printer.

Trier, February 2004

Bernd von Hoffmann

I. MULTILATERALISM AND UNILATERALISM AFTER THE IRAQ CONFLICT

Meinhard Schröder

THE STATUS OF PUBLIC INTERNATIONAL LAW SEEN FROM A EUROPEAN PERSPECTIVE

I. Perceptions and Positions

1. The national and international public paid remarkably high and unprecedented attention to the compliance with international norms in the Iraq crisis as well as to the consequences of the US unilateral action for the future of international law. The reasons for this awareness are the following:
   a) As a consequence of an *institutional understanding*, determining and developing the international community mainly through cooperation by states in international organisations, in particular the United Nations, all peacekeeping and peacemaking decisions have to be made within these organisations and have to be based on their rules and principles.[1]
   b) Because of the historical experiences made by the European states, preference is given to diplomatic means of dispute settlement instead of *using force*; the establishment of high standards for the use of force, especially by restricting self-defence and excluding preemptive measures, derives from this concern.[2]
   c) Special attention is given to US foreign policy deriving from the military-logistic potential of the US and their singularity as the only remaining superpower after the worldwide change.[3]
2. Against this background the military intervention in Iraq has frequently been regarded as a defeat of international law and an origin for an expected or welcomed change in the world order.
   a) To a large extent the intervention has been regarded as a breach of *international law* as not being based on a UN mandate but instead

---

* The author wishes to thank Verena Meyer for her cooperation in preparing this paper.

1 *Krause, J.*, Multilaterale Ordnung oder Hegemonie?, in: Aus Politik und Zeitgeschichte, B 31-32/2003, p. 6 (7-8).

2 *Stoiber, E.*, Europa und die Konzepte für eine neue Weltordnung, in: Tutzinger Blätter, Informationen aus der Ev. Akademie Tutzing, 3/2003, p. 4 (5).

3 See *de Beer, P.*, Conflits: le nouvel ordre américain, in: Le Monde Dossiers et Documents, No. 322 Juillet-Août 2003, p. 1.

on a problematic security strategy, accusing Iraq of possessing weapons of mass destruction and supporting terrorist groups, and as inconsistent with the prohibition of the use of military force. The change of regime has been the ultimate cause.

b) Furthermore this breach sets a precedent constituting an event of war in the cause of a violent overthrow which – until now – had been regarded as off limit under international law.[4] Wars which aim at improving the world no longer need justification. The futile UN human rights policy is replaced by unilateral measures as demonstrated by the US.[5]

c) The breach of international law appeared to be symptomatic for an expected unipolar, US-dominated world order in which international law and multilateral measures are restricted by national interest. Proof for such US unilateralism can be found in the handling of the Rome statute and the Kyoto protocol, the unilateral economic sanctions and the treatment of the Guantanamo prisoners[6] – a US unilateralism thoughtless of the international system.[7]

3. The experiences of the war against Iraq have produced different strategies:

   a) In the light of existing international law, importance should be attached to the European Union and it should gain more importance, to confront the hegemonic unilateralism of the US.[8] The European foreign and security policy has to reflect the anti-imperialistic and pluralistic European traditions, which find their analogy in the principles and foundations of the UN Charter. The governments of the

---

4 See *Lesnes, C.*, L'adieu à l'internationalisme, in: Le Monde (N 3), p. 2.

5 See *Habermas, J.*, Was bedeutet der Denkmalsturz? in: FAZ No. 91 (2003), p. 33.

6 See *Tomuschat, Chr.*, Der selbstverliebte Hegemon, in: Internationale Politik 58 (2003) Issue No. 5, p. 39 (42-44); *Hippler, J.*, Unilateralismus der USA als Problem der internationalen Politik, in: Aus Politik und Zeitgeschichte, (N 1) 15 (16-17).

7 *de Beer*, "un unilatéralisme musclé qui ne ménage plus l'architecture juridique internationale"; *de Beer*, La crise de la gouvernance mondiale, in: Le Monde (N 3), p. 2, "le nouveau président américain a aussi pris pour cible l'architecture juridique internationale".

8 See in this context the controversy between *Derrida, J./Habermas, J.*, Unsere Erneuerung. Nach dem Krieg: Die Wiedergeburt Europas, in: FAZ No. 125 (2003), p. 33 and *Starbatty, J.*, Die Halbstarken. Habermas traut Europa zuviel zu, in: FAZ No. 143 (2003), p. 35; *Wehler, H. U.*, Lasst Amerika stark sein, in: FAZ No. 146 (2003) p. 33; see also: *Link, W.*, Das antiimperiale Europa, in: FAZ No. 198 (2003) 8/27, p. 6.

member states should no longer leave the question of war to the US-Americans, dealing only with questions of peace. Otherwise the European Union would resign itself to playing the part of the Athenians in ancient Rome subordinated lastly to the will of a new empire.[9]

b) The demands for a future trend in international law have three dimensions:

(1) Based on the presumption that pre-emptive protection against threats caused by terrorists, possession of weapons of mass destruction and the collapse of states cannot be safeguarded by the right to self-defence – an analysis on which also the US-National Security Strategy is grounded – Article 51 has to be newly adjusted. Retaining to traditional international law would just lead to a loss of authority and cohesion. A renewed conception of international law, however, offers the chance to put the development of the use of force were it belongs – into the sphere of law and international institutions – and thus to preserve world peace.[10]

(2) The principles of state sovereignty, territorial integrity and prohibition of intervention have been questioned as sole parameters for world order: As the right of self-defence, including the right of emergency assistance, and the prohibition of intervention have failed, international law has to be carefully developed. If the concept of sovereignty looses its guiding power, the legitimacy of a decision making process determined by international law gains importance. By this means, the UN's capacity to act needs to be invigorated, the process of integrating international relations into a legal system has to be furthered.[11]

---

9 Statement of the Committee on Foreign Affairs of the EP (Report of the new European security and defence architecture – priorities and deficiencies (2002) 2165 (INI)), p. 16 adopted 2003/4/10 in plenary session of the EP. See also in this context: *P. Bender*, Weltmacht Amerika. Das neue Rom. 2003.

10 *Stoiber* (N 2).

11 See Beschluss des CDU-Bundesverbandes of 28th April 2003, Part 7, in: FAZ No. 104 (2003/5/6), p. 9 and *Ignatieff, M.*, Warum sind wir im Irakkrieg?, Addition to the magazine "Kommune" 1/2004, p. IX et seq.; see also *Kissinger, H.*, Does America Need a Foreign Policy: Toward a Diplomacy for the 21st Century, 2002, p. 234, 2002, "These innovations reflect the new conventional wisdom, according to which tradi-

(3) Considering that the preventive abatement of threats is a duty of the international community, a reform of the composition of the Security Council and the use of the veto is being discussed as well as a reform of the instruments.[12]

II. Controversial Appraisals of the International Legal System

Controversial appraisals about the relevance and tendencies of the development of international law form the background of those perceptions and positions.

1. International law, strategy of the weak

From the perspective of a state wanting to make use of its unique military power to defend and promote freedom at any time, the notion of giving international law priority over the use of armed force, seduction over coercion, multilateralism over unilateralism may seem as an expression of weakness. The Europeans are reproached with such a weakness: they are not in the position, separately or jointly, to carry out military actions, they turned away from power and are living in a post-historical paradise of peace and prosperity, resembling the realization of Kant's perpetual peace. Reality however is perceived to be different. According to this view, the United States use their power in an anarchical, Hobbesian world. International law is not reliable as long as true security, defence and promotion of a peaceful order are now as ever dependent on the possession and the use of military power.[13]

From the European perspective, as well as from the perspective of the whole international community, the prescribed contrast is not acceptable. International law is not just a weapon of the weak to whom other means are not available. It embodies, as an outcome of legal development and world-historical experience, values and principles allowing military use of force – even if serving freedom – only within the scope of existing rules. Whether these rules are still reliable in the light of new threats can therefore not be de-

---

tional principles of sovereignty and noninterference in the domestic affairs of other countries are the principal obstacles to the universal rule of peace and justice."

12 *Tomuschat* (N 6), p. 45-46; *Chancellor Schröder* at the opening session of the 58th UN General Assembly Session: www.un.org/webcast/ga/58/statements/germeng030924.htm; *Gerhardt, V.*, Macht im Recht, Merkur No. 651 (2003), p. 557 (565-568); *Ignatieff* (N 11).

13 *Kagan, R.*, Of Paradise and Power. America and Europe in the New World Order, 2003, p. 3, 38, 55, 73.

cided by single states on their own to gain freedom of action. Nor can the acceptance of international law be made dependant upon its conformity with democratic issues as perceived by the US-American conception.[14] Otherwise it would turn into a form of external constitutional law ("Aussenstaatsrecht")[15] of more or less powerful states. The insistence of the Europeans on the adherence to international law in the war against Iraq is to be understood against this background.

2. *Impact of a breach of international norms*

The statement that the US action in the war against Iraq constitutes a breach of international norms is based upon the assumption that the UN Charter, giving the UN Security Council the primary responsibility for peace and security and restricting violent action against single states to cases of self-defence, was and still is legally binding. On the other hand a "realistic approach" to the use-of-force provisions in international affairs is willing to declare them dead for incontrovertibly having been breached again and again since 1945.[16] In consequence, this implicates that unilateral breaches could deprive an international norm of its binding force.[17] This perception is unacceptable: obligations deriving from customary law or from treaty cannot be abrogated by unilateral action but only by *actus contrarius*. Such an act is not detectable in this case and cannot be established just because the exact borders of a legitimate use of force may be contentious in detail. Since the prohibition of the use of force is *ius cogens*[18], the consensus of the international community underlying this legal norm could only be abrogated under especially high requirements.

Recorded as *interim findings: The international use-of-force provisions have lost their function as standards neither before nor after the war against Iraq.*

---

14 In this sense: *Rubenfeld, J.* (Yale Law School), "Unilateralism and Constitutionalism", speech delivered at the UniDem seminar: European and American Constitutionalism, 23 and 24 May 20003, Göttingen.

15 Notion to be found in: *Hegel*, Grundlinien der Philosophie des Rechts, §§ 330 et seq.

16 Details in: *Morgenthau, H. J.*, Politics Among Nations, 4th ed. 1967, p. 269 et seq.; *Steiner, H. J.*, International Law, Doctrines and Schools of Thought in the Twentieth Century, in: EPIL Vol II (1995), p. 1216 (1225); recently: *Glennon, M.*, Why the Security Council Failed, Foreign Affairs, 2003, p. 16, 22.

17 *Frowein, J. A.*, Ist das Völkerrecht tot?, in: FAZ No. 168 (2003), p. 6; *Bruha, Th.*, Irak-Krieg und Vereinte Nationen, Archiv des Völkerrechts 41 (2003), p. 295 (299-300).

18 See *Ipsen, K.*, Völkerrecht, 4th ed. 1999, 15-55, 59; *K. Doehring*, Völkerrecht, 1999, 4-300.

The US has not questioned in principle the binding power of the provisions. They only deemed themselves justified after the Security Council did not decide in favour of their opinion.

3. Categories to characterize the international legal order after war against Iraq

The statement that the US violated international law through their action, does not tell anything about the efficacy of international law in general. Such generalizations are due to a common selective perception, fading out large spheres of international law where obligation and cooperation between states are smooth and improperly equating single breaches with the collapse of international law as a whole.[19]

Nevertheless *a breach of the use-of-force provisions by the United States has its own quality.* After the worldwide change in 1989/90, the US remains the only superpower with the appropriate military and logistic capability. Their attitude towards the rules of the Charter is of special importance. Marginalizing the UN in connection with the disposability of defining the legitimacy of the use of force is – if consolidated – a possible source of worry and is able to unsettle the foundations of the current international order.[20] Reflections on the future status and possible reform of international law are therefore feasible.

As far as these reflections are tied to a characterization of international law as a *confrontation of unilateralism and multilateralism*, they are problematic. Expecting unilateral action to replace multilateral decisions as a result of the US action in the Iraq crisis is, above all, again a selective consideration adjusted to the rules of war and peace. It will only gain legally relevant powers of persuasion, if multilateral cooperation fails in the longer run. This, however, cannot be predicted definitely. Resolution 1511 (2003) of the Security Council demonstrates clearly that the US, while claiming a major role as occupying power, are dependent on multilateral, UN-mediated cooperation in restructuring a post-war order in Iraq. The similar will apply for the fight against global terrorism. Apart from that, it will be difficult to presume an increasing tendency to unilateral actions for international law as a whole. International law has for a long time allowed unilateral acts besides multilateral cooperation in international organisations, on state conferences and within the framework of treaties. Each form of action has its own conditions and prerequisites. These requirements might be neglected, but this would not cause a

---

19 *Frowein* (N 17).

20 *Tomuschat* (N 6), p. 39.

shift of the international order towards an increasing expansion of unilateral acts.

Considerable doubts can also be raised as to the *use of the categories unipolar/multipolar to characterize the international law system.* The system of international law is regarded as unipolar because the US is for the present the only remaining superpower and is allowed to determine existence and development of international law, thereby exercising a multilateralism à la carte comparable to a hegemony. However, to assume that the international community as a whole is or could be determined by a superpower oversubscribes reality.[21] There are like-minded interests, for instance with the Arabic/Islamic states, developing countries or the European Union, which could not be controlled *hegemonically.* A multilateralism *à la carte* is also *per se* not violating international law: a general duty to cooperate only exists as far as it is legally determined[22], it does not include sole participation to multilateral treaties (like the Kyoto Protocol or the Statute of Rome), no matter how undesirable an abstention is. If the international order is certified to be increasingly developing into a process of constitutionalization in which the states integrate themselves into multilateral treaty systems serving the interest of the entire international community[23], this, however, is not valid in general. With view on the participation of the UN in this constitutionalization it has to be recalled that the UN – as was rightly said –[24] is "based on a paradigm (the 'Kantian model', hinging on cooperation and the promotion of common meta national values) that is profoundly dissimilar to that prevailing in the world community at large (the "Grotian paradigm", typical of an anarchical society consisting of self-centred actors, each pursuing its short-term interests and scarcely concerned about community values)". Within this conflict of paradigm the United Nations can only be as strong as the decisive powers of the international system want them to be and if the UN meets their interests. This applies especially, but not exclusively for the use of armed force.

---

21 See further in this context *Kennedy, P.*, The Rise and Fall of the Great Powers, 1988, p. 533, stating that no great power has ever managed in history to be permanently ahead of other states, and *Kupchan, Ch.*, Die europäische Herausforderung. Vom Ende der Vorherrschaft Amerikas, 2003.

22 *Wolfrum, R.*, in: *Dahm/Delbrück/Wolfrum*, Völkerrecht, Vol. I/3 (2002), p. 854 et seq.

23 See *Kokott/Doehring/Buergenthal*, Grundzüge des Völkerrechts, 3rd ed., 2003, 2-33-35.

24 *Cassese, A.*, International Law, 2001, p. 293.

III. Legal Basis and Conditions of Unilateral Use of Force

1. Current threats as a starting point for new rules on unilateral use of force

Leaving aside more or less problematic generalizations about the efficiency and the determining factors of international law, the reflections on the status and perspectives of the system of international law should relate to the question which possibilities international law offers to unilaterally react to current threats to the international community by using force and whether new rules are deemed desirable. This does not only correspond the line of argumentation forming the foundation of the US National Security Strategy from September 2002 and all statements of the Bush administration since then. It also follows the fears which gave rise to the criticized generalizations on the status and development of international law system. Scrutinizing unilateral use of force and propositions for a reform of the Security Council or a change of the foundations of the system of international law such as territorial sovereignty and prohibition of intervention can be considered.

2. Determination of current threats

Determining current threats against which unilateral use of force can be considered on the basis of the US National Security Strategy, there are essentially two manifestations remaining which may also occur combined:

a) *Global terrorism.*[25] The United States remark in the National Security Strategy: While constantly striving "to enlist the support of the international community, we will not hesitate to act alone, if necessary, to exercise our right of self-defence by acting pre-emptively against ... terrorists to prevent them from doing harm against our people and our country ...."

b) Emergence of a few *rogue states.*[26] These states

- "brutalize their own people and squander their national resources for the personal gain of their rulers;
- display no regard for international law, threaten their neighbors, and continuously violate international treaties to which they are party;
- are determined to acquire weapons of mass destruction, along with other advanced military technology, to be used as threats or offensively to achieve the aggressive designs of these regimes;

25 Chapter III, p. 6.
26 Chapter V, p. 13-15.

- sponsor terrorism around the globe; and
- reject basic human values and hate the United States and everything for which it stands".

In relation to these states, the United States following the National Security Strategy are determined to adopt a concept of imminent threat to the capabilities and objectives of today's adversaries. To forestall or prevent such hostile acts by their adversaries, the United States will, if necessary, act pre-emptively.

3. *The use of force consistent with the international law system*

a) As confirmed by Security Council Resolutions 1368 and 1373[27] (2001) terrorist acts count as armed attacks in terms of Article 51 and self-defence is therefore generally legitimised against states offering international terrorists a base of operations or supporting them otherwise.[28] In any case, two questions are still unanswered:

(1) Considering the terrorist network, self-defence can be executed against many states. To keep the use of violence within reasonable limits, which extent of support makes a state a legitimate target for self-defence? Should this decision rest with the attacked state or would it be in better hands with the Security Council?[29]

(2) Measures of self-defence have to be the immediate reaction to an armed attack. From this point of view, the legitimacy and prerequisites of *pre-emptive measures* gain importance. It is true that they are often regarded as being irreconcilable, but this position is not convincing. Following the criteria defined in the Caroline Case, self-defence has to be allowed if terrorist acts of considerable dimension are immediately threatening and any other possibility for defence is exhausted.[30] Claiming this modality, however, would not have been

---

27 ILM 40 (2001), 1277 pp; a detailed and convincing appreciation at: *C. Kreß*, "Strafrecht und Angriffskrieg im Lichte des Falles Irak", ZStW 115 (2003), 294 (318-330).

28 For details: *Cassese, A.*, Terrorism is also Disrupting Some Crucial Legal Categories of International Law, EJIL 12 (2001), 993 (996-997); *Bothe, M.*, Terrorism and the Legality of Pre-emptive Force, EJIL 14 (2003), 227 (230); *Tomuschat*, Der 11. September und seine rechtlichen Konsequenzen, EuGRZ 2001, 535 (538-544).

29 *Cassese* (N 28), p. 997 and 1000.

30 See *Nolte, G.*, Weg in eine andere Rechtsordnung. Vorbeugende Gewaltanwendung und gezielte Tötungen, in: FAZ No. 8 (2003), p. 8; *Tomuschat* (N 6); *Kreß* (N 27), p. 314-315.

possible in the case of the war against Iraq for lack of appropriate evidence and has not been claimed by the US.[31]

b) (1) The use of force against so-called rogue states consistent with the system of international law can be authorized by the *Security Council.* Such authorization existed in the Gulf war in the form of Resolution 687 (1990). It was missing in the war against Iraq; Resolution 1441 (2002) threatened with serious measures but did not authorize their appliance, least of all military measures.

(2) To what extent the *possession of weapons of mass destruction as such* creates a threat appropriate to Article 51 is questionable and may be approved only if special circumstances suggest an immediate effort.[32] Even if these circumstances could be seen in the anti-American attitude and the incalculability of dictator Saddam Hussein, a sufficient proof for the possession of weapons of mass destruction ready for duty in Iraq at all is still lacking.

(3) *Eliminating undesirable regimes in rogue states* can only be achieved on the grounds of a right to self-defence under the described prerequisites however lacking in war against Iraq.

(4) *Humanitarian intervention* in rogue states to protect human rights where they are massively hurt (as practiced in Kosovo) requires a current threat to the people – legal justification for the humanitarian intervention is still controversial[33] – which did not exist in Iraq before the intervention and has neither been claimed to exist by the US.[34]

4. *The concept of pre-emptive strikes within the US National Security Strategy as a concept changing the international law system*

a) The description of possible responsiveness to the attitude of so-called rogue states in the US National Security Strategy bluntly abandons existing law: The so far decisive criteria of imminent threat shall be left obsolete, pre-emptive use of force legitimised offhand namely through assumed abstract threats emanating from rogue states. It is without doubt that this propagates a system-changing concept of unilateral use of force.

---

31 Correctly: *Kreß* (N 27), p. 313-314.
32 *Sofaer, A. D.*, On the Necessity of Pre-emption, EJIL 14 (2003), 209 (221-223).
33 Discussed at *Wolfrum* (N 22), p. 829.
34 Correctly: *Kreß* (N 28), p. 316-317.

It can and has to be discussed whether this concept marks the beginning of a desired development in international law. The answer depends essentially on the implications for the system of international law. The pre-emptive use of force conspicuously cuts the threshold for the unilateral use of force. The perception of the state determined to use pre-emptive force decides about rogue states and the threats emanating from them. An independent control is regularly not possible, least of all pre-emptively.[35] Usually, the same also applies for the determination of an imminent threat within the scope of a right to self-defence; an increase in the pre-emptive use of force would essentially broaden uncertainty for the international community. To the extent abstract threats are deemed to be able to justify the use of pre-emptive force, it is barely distinguishable, when, by whom and against which state armed force will be used.[36] Since the use of force always also violates foreign sovereignty and territorial integrity, the concept at the same weakens time the foundations of the international law system.

b) The foundations of international law are also challenged by the concept from the angle of fundamental rules of the UN Charter.[37] Following Art. 39 it is the duty of the international community represented by the Security Council, not of single states, to meet threats to the peace like those being described in the US National Security Strategy if necessary through a – as German chancellor *Schröder* said at the UN General Assembly – "comprehensive prevention"[38]. In estimating the mischief the members of the Security Council certainly carry heavy responsibility. They must take those concerns seriously and show that these issues can and will be addressed effectively through collective action.[39] This includes balancing whether or not to carry out military actions against a state neglecting obligations under international law. It is *part of the system* to have to deal with different opinions finally being determined (as before the war against Iraq) by the attitude of the Security Council's members to the use of force in principal and in a precise case (for instance as a result of historical experiences). If no decision to use armed force can be made, even

35 *Nolte* (N 30); *Murswiek, D.*, Die amerikanische Präventivkriegsstrategie und das Völkerrecht, NJW 2003, 1014 (1018-19); *Ignatieff* (N 11), p. IV.

36 *Nolte* (N 30).

37 *Tomuschat* (N 6), p. 45-47.

38 To be found at: www.un.org/webcast/ga/58/statements/germeng030924.htm.

39 In this sense Secretary-General, Kofi Annan, statement at the opening session of the 58th UN. www.un.org/webcast/ga/58/statements/sg2eng030923.htm.

the states approving such measures must leave it at this. A right to self-defence compliant with international law still remains, if the prerequisites are available.

c) Secretary-General *Kofi Annan* said at the opening session of the 58th UN General Assembly Session that the United Nations was in a very bad constitution.[40] This statement cannot refer to the instruments used to pre-emptively combat the threats to the peace and to international security, but rather only to the willingness of the states to act collectively in the framework of the United Nations. The existing instruments of the Security Council are widespread enough to face even novel types of threats. Propositions to reform the composition of the Security Council or the use of the veto can render the circle of states, carrying a special responsibility for peace and international security, more representative. But they are not appropriate to provide the pre-emptive combat of threats to the peace and to international security with greater efficiency, not mentioning their realisability.[41]

   Propositions wanting to reform Art. 51 or putting into question the concept of sovereignty respectively territorial integrity or the principle of non-intervention do likewise not contribute to an advancement of international law. They weaken the collective responsibility of the international community and endanger the indispensable foundations of international law.

d) To keep as a result: The concept of pre-emptive action does not provide a positive approach for the development of international law. The pre-emptive use of force remains a task to be coped with on the basis of the existing rules of the UN Charter; a reform is not required. A breach of these rules however, like in the war against Iraq, cannot be obviated for the future. The development of a European common foreign and security policy cannot change this in principal. Uniformed positions may, however, help to defend and protect the legal foundations of the Charter. This is anything but an outmoded perception of Europe.

---

40 Ibid.

41 Also sceptical: *Tomuschat* (N 37).

MICHAEL J. GLENNON

THE UN'S IRRELEVANT RELEVANCE*

02 July 2003 In the aftermath of the UN Security Council's disastrous breakdown over Iraq, the system's usual apologists have reemerged, arguing, once again, that the Security Council has established its "relevance." The refrain is by this time familiar: the United States was forced by world opinion, we are told, to go to the Council on Iraq; the United States needed to approach the Council, like Henry IV seeking out Pope Gregory VII in Canossa, to garner legitimacy; the Council's lifting of sanctions against Iraq demonstrates that it is "back in the game." God is in his heaven, in other words, and all's right with the world. The international security system works.

In assessing this claim it is useful to start with the United Nations' own statement of the standard by which its system is to be judged. The standard is not "relevance." The standard is set out in ringing words in the opening provision of the UN Charter. The objective, the Charter states, is to "save succeeding generations from the scourge of war." To this end, it establishes the Security Council, the purpose of which is to "maintain international peace and security."

By its own standard, the system has failed. Well over a hundred times since the Charter's framing in 1945, member states have used armed force in flagrant disregard of its prohibition, with no plausible claim that their resort to arms was "in response to an armed attack" – which is the only time force may be used under the Charter without Security Council approval. Most recently, NATO's then-19 member states representing 780 million people engaged in the aerial bombing of Yugoslavia without the faintest claim that their act was defensive. And they did so, of course, without even approaching the Security Council for approval, for it was widely recognized that Russia, and perhaps China as well, would veto any proposed intervention to stop ethnic cleansing in Kosovo.

What is the legal significance of this sorry record? We might begin by reminding ourselves that the international legal system is different from domestic legal systems. The international system is voluntarist. Unlike individuals who are subject to domestic law, states are bound only to observe those rules with which they have consented to comply. An individual can hardly reject the pro-

---

* This article by Professor Glennon also appeared in the Frankfurter Allgemeine Zeitung (FAZ), Germany, under the German title "Der Traum", No. 144 (2003), p. 7.

hibition against robbing banks and thereby exempt himself from that rule's application. But a state that rejects a rule is on a different footing because states, in the international system, are both the objects and the makers of the law. States are not bound to rules to which they do not consent.

How do we know to what rules states have consented? At the outset the process is simple: we look at their words, which states embody in treaties. But practice also conveys intent, in states as with individuals. And when practice is later in time and comprised numerous acts of multiple states over many years, we are well to heed those acts as a truer indicium of state intent than words of an earlier era.

Thus it hardly takes an international law scholar to realize that the infamous Kellogg-Briand Pact of 1928 – by which every major belligerent in World War II committed itself to foregoing war as an instrument of national policy – has long been a dead letter. It is no accident that North Korea today so insistently seeks a non-aggression pact with the United States. If the UN Charter were still good law, North Korea would of course require no such assurance to protect itself from an American attack, for the Charter was intended to be the mother of all non-aggression pacts, precluding for all time the need for states to seek such assurances. But who seriously would advise the North Koreans today that they need no non-aggression pact with the United States because the UN Charter protects them?

The Charter, tragically, has gone the way of the Kellogg-Briand Pact. It has fallen into desuetude, having been superseded by state practice altogether inconsistent with its lofty ideals. It has been overtaken by the atavistic violence that has defeated efforts of states to define the crime of aggression that is set out in the statute of the International Criminal Court – which the Court is some day expected to prosecute and punish. The harsh reality is that there is no consensus today among states as to when use of force is appropriate.

This fundamental philosophical difference is one key reason for the breakdown of the Security Council in dealing with Iraq. Another is the fact of American unipolarity and the incentives that unipolarity generates. France, Russia, and China have in recent years undertaken as a central objective of their foreign policy to return to a world of multipolar configuration of power. Germany has itself recently become a party to this project. The United States, on the other hand, is irrevocably committed to maintaining a unipolar world. The national security strategy statement adopted last fall said that "[o]ur forces will be strong enough to dissuade potential adversaries from pursuing a military build-up in hopes of surpassing, or equaling, the power of the United States." It can come as no surprise that a collision occurred in the Security

Council: America and its power competitors are committed to incompatible long-term strategic goals. Each uses the Security Council (as well as other international institutions such as NATO) as an instrument for seeking to advance that goal. When the lever is pulled in opposite directions, the result is predictable: paralysis.

A third force, lingering for years in NATO, has emerged since the Second Gulf War to afflict broader collective security efforts. That is the so-called "free-rider" phenomenon. This describes the tendency of states, like individuals, to avoid doing their proportionate share when another actor is willing to do more. This phenomenon has loomed large in efforts to resolve the threat of a nuclearized North Korea. States that earlier had excoriated the United States for "unilateralism" suddenly have been nowhere to be found when it comes to joining in an effort to curb North Korea's nuclear program. Their hesitation has been entirely rational: Why expend a state's treasure, let alone expose its people to apocalyptic risk, when another state is willing to undertake the entire burden itself? This is the situation in which the United States increasingly finds itself as "policeman of the world." The more the United States acts unilaterally to provide collective security, the smaller the incentive provided other states to participate.

These are some, though not all, of the reasons why the UN's system of collective security has failed. These forces are exogenous to the architecture of the United Nations; they do not flow from design flaws within the organizational structure of the Security Council. Rather, they are structural characteristics of the international system, features of the way states behave in a system with no centralized authority. Accordingly, remedies directed at "fixing" the UN blueprint by, for example, adding more developing states to the Security Council, or by diluting the power of the veto accorded the permanent five members of the Council – these solutions miss the point. The problems lie not within the architecture of the United Nations but within the dynamics of the state system. The ground on which such an edifice must stand is not yet ready to support it. The preconditions necessary for creating a functioning legalist regime to control the use of force are not present.

This is the discouraging response that must be made to those who demand that the realists present an alternative solution. Within the legalist paradigm, there is no solution: the current institution cannot work, nor can any alternative work. The Council's recent lifting of sanctions against Iraq, while a welcome step toward reconciliation, hardly presents a counter-example. Constrained by the need to restore contractual integrity to Iraqi oil sales, the United States did not have the legal option of avoiding the Council, as it had earlier, nor did its

European power competitors have the political option of blocking that action and taking the blame for continued Iraqi civilian suffering.

The question on which policy-makers might most usefully focus, therefore, is not how the operation of the Security Council can be improved. Given the structural limitations it confronts, improvements in performance can be only marginal. Rather, the question is how a given state can most effectively recalibrate its foreign policy to protect its national interest under conditions of unipolarity.

As long-standing relationships are re-thought in this new light, an immediate instinct of some European policy-makers will be to attempt to use those international institutions in which the United States participates to check American power, as did France, Russia and Germany in the Security Council prior to the recent war. In the short term, such "coming-of-age" initiatives may on occasion succeed. However, the long-term consequence will simply be to instill in American policy-makers an incentive to go it alone. There is, after all, no reason why a state that seeks to enhance its power – meaning simply its ability to get what it wants – should submit to seemingly avoidable limits. Any nation would chafe at the thought of doing so (as did the French at the prospect of having their own multipolarist project undercut by uppity "New Europe" last year). Far-sighted German statesmen, therefore, will be prudent in attempting to enlist international institutions in the effort to get a leg up on the United States, however "emancipating" the immediate result. Ultimately, unless "victory" is defined as forcing the United States to pull back from participating in international institutions, such efforts will be self-defeating.

A more productive approach will lie in understanding more precisely the dynamic that generates contemporary American ambivalence towards international institutions. Because of its preponderant power, U.S. policy-makers now confront a paradox. On the one hand, they must avoid getting locked into a situation in which the United States needs the legitimacy that an institution can confer in order to act effectively. There is no point in being a "hyper power" if no significant foreign policy initiative can be implemented without the concurrence of other states. On the other hand, the legitimacy to be conferred by international institutions can, at least in some circumstances, clearly advance American interests. Legitimacy concerns thus pull American policy-makers in opposite directions.

These are only short-term considerations. Conflicting long-term interests make America's calculation even more difficult. The likelihood is that American hegemony will not last forever. Accordingly, it makes sense for the United States to commit itself to at least some international institutions, rules and regimes so that its interests can be protected when its relative advantage in hard power has faded. (Included within the notion of "advantage" is both capability and will: a dozen carrier battle groups provide no power advantage at all absent a continued willingness to use them.) Weighing against such a commitment, however, is the risk of doing so prematurely, of subjecting American power to multilateral restraints before America's relative power advantage actually begins to wane. Striking the proper balance requires making just the right empirical guess as to how history will unfold – a daunting task for policy-makers in any country.

These considerations suggest that the long trans-Atlantic debate over unilateralism versus multilateralism is misdirected. These are false categories. In many circumstances, these modes of behavior are mutually reinforcing rather than oppositional. Unilateralism can, for example, sometimes enable multilateralism, as it did last winter when the threat of an American attack led Iraq to accept a strict new inspections regime under the auspices of the Security Council. The Security Council benefited from the American threat of unilateral force. In a broader context, American unilateral military might can surely be credited in part with having provided a realm of security within which European integration flourished during the second half of the 20th Century, as *Robert Kagan* has noted. Multilateralism, similarly, is often directed at expanding the latitude of unilateralism. This is particularly true for the United States. Working with other states softens the jagged edges of American hegemony, breeding less resentment than coercion and bullying. It is far more effective to cause other governments to want what the United States wants than to force them, against their will, to do what the United States wants. Cooperation and consultation, when possible, will prolong American hegemony and make it possible for the United States to act alone when it believes it needs to.

Sensible American policy-makers will therefore realize that the correct question is not whether a given initiative is unilateral or multilateral, but whether it advances American interests. This judgment should be made pragmatically, not ideologically. The outcome must be context-dependent, varying with the facts of each case. The Bush Administration was by this standard correct in moving against Afghanistan without Security Council approval; it ill behooves a superpower to seek international approval to respond to an armed attack on its own citizens and territory. Such an action would have led other states to expect American submission to the United Nations in other, future instances where the United States' legitimate interest lies in uncircumscribed freedom of action. In contrast, American policy-makers have been mistaken in resisting the return of UN weapons inspectors to Iraq. The United States has an interest in being believed. If and when weapons of mass destruction are found in Iraq, American credibility will be enhanced by the presence of UN weapons inspectors at their side, able to authenticate American claims. (Moreover, given its earlier experience in Iraq, the International Atomic Energy Agency may be better able to safeguard the security of Iraqi nuclear materials than can the United States acting alone.)

Pragmatism also counsels American policy-makers to tone down the hyperbolic rhetoric of good and evil. Their repeated insistence upon "moral clarity" in the wars against terrorism and Iraq, like the insistence that other nations are "either for us or against us," suggests a world of black and white rather than the multiple shades of gray that characterize all great moral questions. American success in the Cold War was due in no small part to its willingness to recognize that many nations were "for us" in some ways but quite "against us" in others. The United States itself made common cause with myriad tyrants on a theory of lesser evil. Today's clarion call of moral purity, suggesting a perfect American identity with the forces of light, no doubt had political utility following September 11 in rallying Americans to the support of their country. There is no shortage of patriotism in the United States today, however, and it would be more useful for the Administration to recognize that many of the issues confronted by the United States and its allies are questions on which reasonable persons can differ. "Every difference of opinion," Thomas Jefferson said, "is not a difference of principle."

One unfortunate upshot of the recent surge in moralistic rhetoric has been the increased resort to systems of validation other than law. Alternative validating systems include notions of legitimacy, justice, natural law and the like. As contrasted with law, such systems present two weaknesses. First, none is based upon consent, which is the element of law that renders it applicable to all actors within a given universe. Only law is truly universal. Second, none is objective. Each lies in the eye of the beholder. However powerful the surrounding rhetoric, claims of "legitimacy" have no objective force; "legitimacy" and "justice" are constructs of the human mind, not something out there, waiting to be discovered. As a result, power and preference underpin these alternative validating systems, which are ultimately products of the same cultural variables that account for the attitudinal divide that has beset legalist efforts to manage the use of force.

There is, in the end, therefore, no alternative to law. Under current conditions, however, humanity's efforts to subject the use of force to the rule of law will prove unavailing. But to relent in those efforts would be a great mistake. Cultures will eventually converge worldwide, as they have in Europe. That dream will one day be realized globally. In the meantime, our aim today must be to ensure that that day is not unnecessarily delayed. Pretending that the current system successfully subjects the use of force to the rule of law can result only in unnecessary delay.

HANNS W. MAULL

GLOBALISATION, POLITICS AND THE STATE

Although the dynamics of globalisation at first glance seem driven by technological innovation and markets, at its core globalisation is a political project, promoted by states and through co-operation and competition between states. Yet politics are also profoundly affected by globalisation, and as a result both the state and the international system of governance have come under tremendous pressure to adapt. The way in which states and world politics will adjust to the new circumstances brought about by the dynamics of globalisation will shape the future of globalisation: it will thus remain at heart a political process. This does not necessarily mean, however, that politics will be able to control globalisation. If we compare the world of globalisation to a car speeding along a winding road, politics is behind the steering wheel, the brakes and the accelerator. Yet there are many different ways of trying to control the car, and there are many drivers behind the wheel who may interfere with each other. Similarly, there are many different ways in which politics could shape globalisation in the future.

I. What is Globalisation?

Globalisation is, as a US diplomat once put it, the present state of world affairs where "everything is connected with everything else, only more so". Contrary to a widespread misunderstanding, globalisation therefore is not only, and not even primarily, about transnational production networks, global finance, or the IT revolution. It is all-encompassing: it affects and changes everything, including, of course, ourselves.

What globalisation is, and how it can be measured

Globalisation is a process of all-encompassing social change. It unfolds along the dimensions of space and time (where it can be measured by changes in the *extensity* and *intensity* (i.e., by changes in the geographic reach and the magnitudes of interactions across borders), and in their *velocity* and *impact* (i.e. by changes in the speed of interactions and their reverberations) and along the dimension of social organisation: different stages of globalisation can be distinguished by differences in *infrastructure* (the channels and means through which interaction is carried out), *institutionalisation* (the institutions associated with it), *stratification and distribution of resources* (such as power, wealth or status) between those who are inter-connected, and *modes of interaction* (for example, the predominance of empires or city-states, of military force or trade, of international strive or peaceful co-operation).

Globalisation is not a new phenomenon. The silk and spice trade between Asia and Europe along the silk road and by way of sea was of great importance in medieval economic life, and transcontinental economic flows between Latin America, Europe and Asia were at the core of European economies in the 16th and 17th century: gold and silver from the Spanish colonies ultimately paid for European imports of silk and spices from Asia, financing Europe's perennial trade deficits with the latter. Agricultural products were introduced across long distances in new continents, changing patterns of production and consumption. The medieval plague, which devastated Europe from the 13th and 14th centuries onward, originated in Asia and first reached Europe aboard a ship bound for Venice which carried East Asian spices – and rats infested with the bacteria.

Globalisation is thus not a state of affairs but a process with a long history. Of course, the thickening, over time, of cross-border transactions and its dramatic acceleration in recent years do not form straight lines but a series of advances and retreats. Yet the process is "directed" – that is, it develops within a corridor of possibilities determined by the past and by the characteristics of those processes themselves. And while in one sense it represents but a new phase in a long chain of historical evolutions, from another perspective globalisation has entered a qualitatively new era since the late 1970s. This new quality is the result of

- the unparalleled extensity and intensity of interconnections between societies in all spheres of life,
- the speed of change, and above all
- the rise of technological capabilities to destroy civilization (e.g. through nuclear war), modify the world climate and genetically change human beings.

In sum, the present stage of globalisation is marked by enormous complexity and turbulence (in the sense of mathematical chaos theory). This gives rise to the question: who is in charge of the process? And: how can it be kept under control?

II. Globalisation and Politics: How the State Sustains Globalisation ...

Who or what drives globalisation? Most basically, human ambition and ingenuity. The foundations to the modern age were laid in the Middle Ages with the rise of scientific inquiry and rationality, the (re-)discovery of the individual and the spirit of "can do". In terms of social institutions, the two main promoters of globalisation have been markets and war between states. Globalisation is often seen as the consequence of technological innovation and market dynamics, but this view neglects the important role of politics and political ideas. At its heart, globalisation is a political project. States have pushed globalisation forward in their search for economic and military advantages, not least vis-à-vis their competitors. But they were also profoundly affected by the process: earlier phases of globalisation have led, through evolution, to the rise of the modern nation state (and, eventually, the democratic welfare state) as the historically most powerful form(s) of political organisation so far.

States (or more precisely, those who act in their name) are powerful because their decisions command authority: its people are willing to adjust their behaviour in line with what the state tells them, even if they do not believe in the merit of the state's decision and cannot expect material rewards (in fact, they may well be asked to give money to the state or even risk their lives in its service). This authority of the state rests on two sources: on the ability to enforce its decisions against resistance through sanctions, and on the legitimacy of the state, that is, the willingness of its people to follow the state out of a general sense of loyalty and appropriateness.

The exercise of this authority is called "governance": the term describes how a collective tries to secure its future and achieve its aspirations. It derives from the Latin/Greek words for "steering" – i.e. steering a car towards the desired destination. Determining the course and steering a society and a country is the job of "the government". At the level beyond the state, it is the interaction of states with each other (and with other, transnational actors such as business or NGOs) which determines the course of international society; this interaction, and the resulting patterns and institutions, are what we call "global governance".

At its most basic, the state should provide protection of its citizens against nature and violence. This, in turn, requires military power and economic wealth. From the beginning, the state therefore has been involved both in organising violence and in organising economic production, e.g. through the provision of infrastructure (such as irrigation, storage, and lines of transportation, but also through laws). Beyond those core functions, states provide a range of public goods, they help shape social and economic life through laws and regulations, and they determine the distribution of wealth, income and status.

What states do on their own territory, and what they do in co-operation or in their struggle with others, has profound implications for globalisation. The shape of globalisation would be completely different without the state and the state system: there would be no currencies, no trade barriers, no real wars (but probably still much violence). More specifically, the present stage and specific appearances of globalisation cannot be explained without recourse to a range of crucial political decisions, such as the establishment and gradual advancement of an open, liberal world economic order (the Bretton Woods system) under American tutelage and, more recently, of the liberalisation of private international capital flows. This major shift in international economic governance initially was promoted by the governments of the US and the UK for essentially domestic reasons through a series of policy innovations. The process gained momentum through the rise of neo-liberalist ideas and the pressure on other states to follow the liberalisation measures of America and Britain. The development of the internet also illustrates the critical role of the state in the evolution of globalisation: the net arose out of a research project funded by the US Defence Department; the crucial communication protocols which set the standards enabling the development of the net were set in a series of contracts between the US government and university research centres. Although the internet today has been completely privatised, states continue successfully to regulate internet content.

III. ... and How it is Changed by Globalisation

Globalisation thus is the product of state policies, and the interaction of states in a system of global governance. But globalisation also has profoundly affects the state – or more precisely, on each state individually, on the way states function in general, and on their interaction in the system of global governance.

The principal impact of globalisation at this stage on the state is to undermine its territorial and social cohesion and its political authority. Boundaries become porous and permeable, and people's loyalties become more diffuse and multi-faceted. States find it more difficult to control and tax their citizens, because they can more easily evade the state's reach or resist its demands. Equally, states find it harder to control and tax economic activity on their territory.

The implications of those changes should not be exaggerated. First, most economies still are surprisingly "national". Secondly, in a formal sense, state sovereignty is not under threat, it remains completely unchallenged. What is happening is not an erosion of states' juridical sovereignty, but of their autonomy and their ability to regulate and control what is happening on their territory. The idea of the state still survives, enabling the state to command authority and loyalty.

Still, globalisation already has made governance more difficult both for the state and at the international level, and it will almost certainly continue to do so. This is because there is, on the one hand, greater demand for political action to secure what people expect; on the other hand, globalisation complicates the task of realizing those demands. This gap between capabilities and expectations is putting political systems at all levels – nationally and internationally – under pressure. On top of this, states have also been subjected to stronger external influences, from world financial markets, but also from an increasingly vociferous transnational society expecting states to live up to their obligations under international law.

In reality, the universe of states is, of course, vastly diverse. We distinguish a new "Third World" of states, which have not even fully developed the institutions of the modern nation-states, a new "Second World" of defective nation-states, and a new "First World" of states, which have by and large been successful in establishing themselves as modern nation-states, but now have to adapt towards a new, post-modern environment.

1. Quasi-states, failed and failing states

Many ex-colonies of the West, and of the former Russo-Soviet empire, have been "quasi-states" in that sense: they enjoyed all the legal paraphernalia of modern nation states, but only part of its substance. Some of those, such as several West African states, the Congo or Somalia, have fallen apart violently: the monopoly of force of the state in its territory, which may not have been assured in the first place, has given way to "new wars", which combine features of civil war with that of external intervention and the transnational commercial organisation of violence. Other states, such as Iraq or North Korea, have been captured by cliques who, through a mixture of shrewd national ideology, co-optation and brutal repression, have "privatised" the state, turning it into their personal fiefdom. In such states, politics turns around tribalism, religion or other forms of identity. State control is ineffective or non-existent, and the monopoly of force has been dissolved: conflicts therefore often degenerate into violence. The economic foundations of those states are found in the exploitation of raw materials (oil, diamonds) and illegal activities (drugs, prostitution) for world markets. They are to be found in enclaves, which often have very limited links with the rest of the economy. International aid plays an important part in sustaining the population of those states, which can or will no longer feed and protect their people.

2. *Defective states*

Another group of states, also often in the "Second" and "Third" World, is trying to adapt, often under external pressure and supervision (which, in economic policies but also increasingly with regard to "good governance", is chiefly conducted by the IMF) its political and administrative system to the new requirements. Many of those states have been in the "third wave" of democratisation, which started in the 1970s and gathered momentum during the late 1980s and 1990s. The transition towards democracy for those countries has been uneven and diverse, however, producing not only successful new democracies (such as Taiwan or South Korea) but also "defective democracies" (such as Russia or several Latin American states), which either seem stuck in a halfway-house or are slipping back into authoritarianism and/or state failure. Politics turn around nationalism and populism, with the exercise of power tied to clientelistic networks, which constrain the administrative competence of the state apparatus. The economic foundations are a mixture of traditional primary industries (agriculture, raw materials) and modern industry, with an often bloated and backward service sector. Again, the economy will be a patchwork of "traditional" and "post-modern" activities, with limited integration between the segments and enclaves.

3. *New industrial states*

A third group of states have successfully mastered the development of a modern state in line with the requirements of the first industrial revolution. The state has been successful in enforcing control over its territory; security policies are geared towards perceived external threats to the state. Politics turn around national identity, nationalism, territorial integrity and respect for sovereignty, and they will often have an authoritarian bend. The state generally will also take an active interest in managing the economy through intervention. The economic foundations of those states are in modern industries. Examples include China, Malaysia, Turkey, South Korea and Mexico.

4. *Mixed states (modern/post-modern)*

A fourth group of countries have taken their adaptation beyond the modern state paradigm. They are in the process of reconstructing the state in line with the post-modern, globalised economy driven by services and knowledge industries, but retain a substantial industrial base. Their politics turn around wealth creation and wealth sustenance; they tend to be (or at least to move towards) multiethnic and multicultural societies. Territorial issues and sovereignty no longer have much practical political relevance, and although traditional security concerns will persist, those states will tend towards cooperative or even collective security policies and regional/global co-operation. Political systems will be open and generally democratic. The state will play an active role in the economy, but confine itself increasingly to regulatory and subsidiary activities (such as the provision of public goods), rather than directly managing the economy. A key economic policy consideration will be, as in the previous group, to attract foreign capital; the state will therefore tend to turn from a "welfare state" to a "competition state". Examples include the US and many other OECD states.

5. *Virtual/post-modern states*

Lastly, we have a group of states which have gone even further in adapting to globalisation. *Richard Rosecrance* calls them "virtual states". Examples include the Netherlands, Belgium, Singapore, or Luxemburg. These states have all but done away with the remnants of the industrial age, and have specialised in developing the modern service and knowledge industries. Their politics closely resemble that of the previous group, but with even more emphasis on the post-modern aspects of multi-ethnicity, multi-culturalism and an orientation towards attracting foreign capital through maximising national competitive advantages.

Successful adaptation of the state to the new environment of globalisation involves both internal restructuring of the state itself (and of its economy and society) and strategies to enhance the state's ability to achieve desired outcomes through international co-operation and competition. This presupposes considerable political and administrative effectiveness of state action – and many states in the Second and Third World do not yet have that capacity. The challenge for those states (categories one and two) therefore consists in building an effective modern nation-state and simultaneously prepare that state for the new environment. The magnitudes of that challenge can be gauged through the process of EU enlargement, which for many new members will entail such a double transition, or from those countries (such as Bosnia, Kosovo or East Timor), which have become de-facto protectorates of the international community. Generally, external involvement (by International Organisations, OECD countries and the NGO and business sectors) in many countries already now plays a substantial role in this double transition, and external support will no doubt continue to be important. At the same time, the tasks of state building from within and without are dauntingly difficult and as yet not well understood. State collapse and international efforts at state building will therefore probably continue to preoccupy international politics.

IV. The Challenge of State-Adaptation ("First" World)

OECD countries and a handful of other countries run by reasonably efficient and resilient states are better placed to adjust to globalisation. But it will not be easy, either, and success (which, in any case, will always only be temporary) is by no means assured. In the OECD world, too, the state will be faced with a decline in its capacity to control developments on its own territory, while at the same time having to confront new demands for corrective action. Its people will want the state to help them secure the new opportunities offered by globalisation, and to protect them against new risks and threats.

The result is a gap between what the state is expected to do, and what it can actually achieve. It needs to find ways to reduce that gap through a mixture of internal and external adaptation. Thus, domestic restructuring can enhance international competitiveness, e.g. through strengthening education, deregulation (which usually also means re-regulation) and liberalisation, as can conservative fiscal policies and the development of a leaner but more effective state apparatus. External adjustment will be about ways to enhance the state's ability to achieve desired outcomes through international and transnational co-operation along three lines of action:

- regional or functional integration in supranational institutions, which assume certain state functions for their member states and thus develop state qualities at a regional or functional level;
- regional, functional or global co-operation between states below the threshold of integration in regional and international institutions and international regimes;
- and co-operation between governments, international organisations and non-governmental actors (such as business, business associations or NGOs) in regional or global public policy networks.

V. The New System of Global Governance

Out of states' individual responses to the new environment of globalisation – be it through successful adaptation or failure – arise the key features of the new system of global governance. Although states are not the only collective actors in international relations (other important actors are international organisations, NGOs, and firms), their interaction with each other will lay the foundations of that system. It need not be an orderly system; in fact, given the turbulent dynamics of globalisation, it is more likely to be messy than orderly. The term "global governance" only describes the efforts to exercise political control over events; in no way does it suggest that these efforts will actually be able to shape the future.

1. Forms of co-operation

Any system of governance relies on three basic mechanisms to influence and co-ordinate people's behaviour: persuasion, incentives, and, thirdly, commands, backed by sanctions. NGOs, markets and the state roughly represent each of those three mechanisms, and the new system of global governance therefore also will be characterised by interaction between states, markets and NGOs.

States co-operate to jointly secure their objectives ad hoc or through institutions. Institutionalised co-operation can be bilateral or multilateral, it can involve extensive transfers of sovereignty, hence supranational integration, or be confined to international treaties and institutions which provide for co-operation and co-ordination, rather than exercising authority themselves. This co-operation may be regionally confined (regionalism, such as in the case of the European Union), functionally specific (e.g. the WTO or the European Bank for Reconstruction and Development) or comprehensive (such as the United Nations). With very few exceptions (such as the EU), in those institutions states will co-operate voluntarily, and thus fully retain their formal sovereignty (though they may commit themselves, and in practice accept, to comply with the rules, norms and procedures of the institutions concerned). This form of co-operation can be called "international" (or, more precisely, inter-state) co-operation and integration. As a rule, decisions will require unanimity, and they will therefore be the result of complex bargaining and *quid-pro-quos*.

But states increasingly also have to accommodate and co-operate with non-state actors, such as business and NGOs. Governments, NGOs and the private sector get together to form regional, functional or global public policy networks, so as to jointly provide certain public goods. Examples include international banking regulations, efforts to combat international money laundering and others. Again, the decisions taken will represent the outcome of bargaining and mutual accommodation.

The new system of global governance thus consists of a myriad of daily interactions between governments, and between governments and societies, across borders. Much of this will be ad hoc, but interactions will also be patterned and institutionalised. Those patterns and institutions often will involve interaction between states, but they need not do so: markets and NGOs in principle are also able to set up and even to enforce rules and norms for behaviour.

2. *Problems of co-operation*

What distinguishes this new system of global governance from the traditional system of state and interstate governance above all is the role of the state: in the old order, the state was the authoritative enforcer of order; in the new system, it needs to negotiate compliance. State functions previously were carried out – more or less effectively – only by the state, while they are now disaggregated and reassembled in highly complex and disembodied fashion, and thus often are taken over by networks of co-operation and international organisations.

The new system thus raises issues of efficiency and effectiveness, but also of legitimacy and identity. It is far from obvious that the new arrangements for governance will be able to meet what probably is a sharply increased demand for order in international relations, and where it does, this may well be at an exorbitant cost, given the very complex and cumbersome mechanisms available. And the exercise of government beyond the reach of individual governments (though well within their collective domain) may also be challenged from a democratic perspective: the chain of legitimation and participation in global governance decisions obviously becomes very long and indirect. Challenges to its legitimacy, however, will further undermine the anyway tenuous authority of the new system of global governance, and thus also tend to further undermine its effectiveness.

The third problem of this new system of global governance concerns its limited possibilities to express collective identities. The state, at least in theory, represents a nation, and thus allows its citizens to identify with a collective, and express collective wishes. Global governance cannot easily do that, and certainly not to the same degree. Without a collective identity, however, politics and governance lose their constituency. Thus, democracy is government by and for the people – but who are the people? Since identity also involves difference, "mankind" will hardly be a persuasive answer. But if the constituency of global governance isn't mankind – who is it? Presumably, the collective of states and of peoples/nations. But how can their distinct collective identities be accommodated and expressed in this new, complex system of global governance?

Put differently, the problems of the new system of global governance turn around three questions: can this system authoritatively guide globalisation? Can it be accepted as legitimate? And can it accommodate and allow expression for diverse identities?

VI. How can Globalisation be made Sustainable?

Globalisation without politics is a chimera. The issue is not whether globalisation will be governed but only how. A weak system of governance could not only do much harm, it would also severely impede globalisation in unfolding its potential benefits, and might well not be politically sustainable.

At present, demand for governance probably grows more rapidly than adaptation of existing governance arrangements. The result is a widening gap between how much ordering will be needed, and how much can be achieved. If that gap continued to grow, globalisation would no longer be controllable. Man would revert to the role of victim, rather than lord, of anonymous forces beyond its reach: in earlier times, nature; in the future, technology and markets.

What can, what does the state do to sustain globalisation? And what more should and could it do? Basically, states – or, more precisely, statehood as the total effect of states acting, individually and jointly –

- provide protection and order/stability/predictability. This is done through deploying specialised instruments (armed forces, police, legal systems and other bureaucracies) in strategies of unilateral defence (or aggression) and deterrence, co-operative or collective security policies internationally, and in efforts to impose "law and order or "democracy and the rule of law" domestically;
- develop, implement, supervise and ensure compliance with rules, norms and regulations,
- negotiate with other actors common norms and specific agreements, and authorise, implement and sanction the results of such negotiations,
- authorise the transfer of sovereignty to international/supranational institutions and organise their empowerment,

- help express and integrate different identities and thus contribute to social cohesion,
- ensure social acceptance and political legitimacy for existing arrangements and their results. This can be achieved through success (delivering promised or expected goods and benefits), through procedure (e.g. participation in elections), through persuasion, through ideology, or through direct intervention and redistribution, and
- manage crises and enhance social stability and predictability.

As we have argued above, to ensure these functions states need to adapt. Specifically, they will not only have to restructure internally but also need to rely increasingly on supranational, international and transnational forms of co-operative governance. State functions will thus have to be disaggregated, disassembled and reassembled in a new geometry of global governance.

VII. Towards a Strategy of Sustainable Globalisation

From this analysis flow a number of conclusions:

- The complex reconstruction of statehood is inevitable and already under way. It needs to be developed in ways which ensure that globalisation be firmly embedded in strong rules yet lightly governed. Important aspects of this are supranationalism and the empowerment of international institutions. This in no way needs to threaten the state itself, but rather critically depends on it.
- The complex reconstruction of statehood should aim for strong but lean statehood. This involves devolution and decentralisation of authority, delegation and empowerment of business and society, transfer of sovereignty and empowerment of international institutions, a clear focus on long-term, strategic priorities, and a willingness to concentrate and shed activities.
- In the complex reconstruction of statehood into a sustainable system of global governance, the state should be seen as the core, as the strategically crucial moderator and arbiter, and it should be promoted as such. The reconstruction of statehood needs to involve the re-conceptualisation and reconstruction of the state as a lean, strong, democratic and social state.
- Such a re-conceptualisation of the state needs to involve an acceptance by society that it has tended to overburden the state. Expectations in and demands on the state thus need to be lowered and focussed, and support for the state needs to be enhanced. This should not be confused with an

abdication of democratic control over the state and vigilance to ensure that it does not abuse its power. Rather, we should remember President Kennedy's famous admonition of his countrymen: "Ask not what your country can do for you, but what you can do for your country".

DISCUSSION

After the presentations of the three speakers, Professor Dr. Gerhard *Robbers* (Trier) opened the discussion by suggesting three controversial points for further debate:

Firstly, whether there hade been a failure of the UN-System, and if so, what would follow from this. Secondly, whether there was a hegemonic power, and if so, what kind of rules were needed for the law of global governance. Would the rule of law still be regarded as a goal in international relations, or would one player who feels above the law be accepted? Would the system of international relations be multilateral, multipolar or unipolar?

Finally, he asked if the rule of law could still be regarded as an option in such a setting. Would the development of terrorism make a difference in the way war is perceived? Is pre-emptive action or humanitarian intervention needed? He also asks for procedures to legitimise a new kind of structure of international relations.

Professor Dr. Paul *Buteux* (Winnipeg) was the first to speak. He wanted to make some remarks concerning terminology. In his opinion there is no "UN system", but a community of different, legally independent international organizations under the UN umbrella.

He remarked that an important question which should be asked before turning to the question of "Who governs?" and which is directly linked to the term governance should be "Who benefits?". Hinting at similarities he perceives between Canadian and European political discourse he argued that the current discussion takes place in a system where people are rich and secure and where people are benefiting from the system. He wondered why people benefiting from the system would want to change it. In his view there are many people who don't benefit from the present situation, but they don't govern.

He then talked about his experiences with the European way of thinking, that impressed him in the following way: people in the EU were increasingly appropriating the word "European" to their own preferences. Germans, for example, now tended to say that they were Europeans. Given this, it remained unclear to him whether the British, the Dutch, the Spanish or especially the people from the Eastern States were "real Europeans".

Finally he remarked that multilateralism would be completely misunderstood if seen as a counter to unilateralism. Multilateralism is a pattern of cooperation which needs a sufficient basis. It is not a counterweight, as this would merely be an alliance against a common threat.

The second participant to speak was Professor Dr. Stefan *Oeter* (Hamburg) who argued that one must be careful not to exaggerate the degree of failure of the system of collective security. The number of 200 conflicts should be corrected to 20-40 interstate conflicts in the last 50 years. This figure could be regarded as the usual number of breaches a legal system has to accept as a side effect. But still, the fact that most of these conflicts ended in failure cannot be attributed to the working of the UN system of collective security, but is due to other causes, especially balance of power structures. Therefore he regarded the core of Professor Michael J. *Glennon*'s (Medford) argument to be valid.

Nevertheless *Oeter* expressed unease about the statement that the UN Charter provision prohibiting the use of force is in desuetude. He argued not to confuse empirical behaviour with normative programs. In this context he referred to an example *Glennon* had given to illustrate his doubts concerning the validity of the prohibition of force in international law: if a group of people decides to join the weight watchers program and in week one of the program signs a "contract" containing the rule not to eat certain kinds of food in order to reduce their weight, but by week three, everybody has returned to their prior eating habits, is the rule agreed upon in week one still in force? According to *Glennon's* view, the rule has lost its validity through the disregard of the participants. *Oeter*, on the other hand, claimed that the members of the weight watchers program would still recognize the obligation following from the document signed at the beginning of the program regardless of the subsequent behaviour, even if they did not act accordingly. But Professor *Oeter* admitted that in Europe scholars of international law often do not resist the temptation of constructing a fictitious world along the lines of their normative beliefs. This legal formalism represented at least as great a danger as a blunt legal realism that creates norms corresponding to its perceptions of the empirical world. The danger then was that there was little emphasis on the issue of implementation of norms. Therefore, *Oeter* expressed his sympathies for the approach taken by *Glennon*. He acknowledged that the norms governing the system of collective security of the UN Charter do not really work.

Oeter judged the Iraq crisis as a sign of crisis of the UN system, because most states relied on the formal prohibition of the use of force but did not do anything to enforce it, especially when Saddam Hussein expelled the UN weapons inspectors in the late 1990s. *Oeter* therefore expressed understanding for the American position even though he sees no justification for U.S. behaviour. In conclusion he said that Europeans also have to acknowlegde turning a blind eye in their legal thinking.

Professor Dr. Christine *Langenfeld* (Göttingen) expressed doubts concerning the statement by *Glennon* that the prohibition of the use of force had fallen into desuetude. She claimed that as an international lawyer she is confronted with the breach of international legal rules every day. She took the example of the prohibition of torture: although it belongs to a very distinguished body of law which is *ius cogens*, many states are practising torture every day. These states, however, would still agree (if asked) that the prohibition of torture is binding international law and that they feel bound by it. So this rule is still in existence although violated every day.

She stated that the U.S.A. when intervening in Iraq did not justify the action using the notion of pre-emptive action but rather relied on the Security Council Resolution No. 1441. So in her view the U.S.A. did not want to put aside the international legal order but tried to find a legal basis for its action against Iraq. This justification is (highly) debatable and was debated, but still there are scholars arguing in favour of such a justification. However, she added that, however, does not accept a justification based on Resolution No. 1441.

Professor Dr. Daniel *Thürer* (Zürich) started his contribution by explaining his idea of what is "European". According to his view, the notion "European" not only represents a way of talking, but certain concepts and ideas such as the "eternal peace" and the rule of law or the tendency of putting things into an order of concepts. According to him, what happened in Europe was a genuine revolution in international relations and this revolution shaped the way of thinking of Europeans.

Thürer then drew the attention to the relevance of NGOs. As the experience at the Rome Conference on the International Criminal Court demonstrates, they can change the climate of an international conference entirely and are obviously a real force in international relations.

Responding to *Glennon*, *Thürer* remarked that *Glennon* started from the idea that the rules governing the use of force had once been binding norms of international law. In the view of the speaker, *Glennon* had not demonstrated clearly when and how exactly these rules had supposedly lost their quality as legal norms. In the absence of formal amendment of the norm or the invocation of the rule of *clausula rebus sic stantibus*, a norm can lose its character as a binding norm under the concept of desuetude only by contrary customary law. He asked for a proof of this appearance of new customary law.

Finally, *Thürer* expressed his doubts about the statement of *Glennon* that those who are in power will always attempt to enhance their power. Looking back at the history of the USA, he found that one could notice enlightened leaders who followed other principles than rational choice. For example the Declaration of Independence explains on what principles of natural law Americans wished to found their state. U.S. President Wilson tried to reshape the whole system of international relations. After the Second World War aspects of power were set aside, and the Marshall Plan and the Nuremberg trial were set up.

Professor Dr. Klaus *Dicke* (Jena) first expressed his assent with the remarks of *Thürer* concerning desuetude. Desuetude can only be accepted when there is acute contradiction to the norm in question. He claimed that the U.S., in violating international law, had always justified their actions in terms of international law, as for example in the case of the Grenada intervention.

He agreed with *Oeter* that it made sense with regard to the Iraq crisis to ask if things would have changed had Europeans acted in a different way. In 1998, France refused to enforce what it had previously agreed upon concerning Iraq. Germany likewise acted contrary to the UN Charter when it announced its refusal to become engaged in Iraq without regard to future UN Security Council resolutions, despite the fact that the members of the UN have agreed to fulfil the obligations under the UN Charter in good faith.

In conclusion, according to the speaker, it is essential to understand what makes international legal norms work. He is not sure whether it is the criterion of enforcement. Commenting on Professor Dr. Hanns W. *Maull*'s remarks that the system of global governance is deficient one should note that the yardstick to measure deficiency is the nation-state. He suggested the principle of association as a guiding principle for global governance comparable to the Westphalian system. He then tried to challenge *Glennon,* wondering how the empirical data on bank robberies in the U.S. has evolved over the last 200 years and how this development could be analysed. *Dicke* expressed his agreement with *Glennon*: a consensus is necessary. But the crucial point in policies is that once a consensus is needed, it has to be created. The effort of policies to organize consensus is, in the view of the speaker, one of the missing links in the presentation of *Glennon.*

Professor Dr. Matthias *Ruffert* (Jena) argued that the starting point of the theoretical basis of *Glennon's* analysis was not convincing. *Glennon* seemed to follow the Hobbesian idea of "*auctoritas non veritas facit legem*" when extracting norms from the empirical data of state behaviour. *Ruffert* claimed that the theoretical level reached in the discussion of international law had evolved beyond this and that *Glennon* was actually regressing. The basis of international law was not the consent of every state with every single rule, but compliance with universal values. He admitted that it may be difficult to describe them and that such an approach gives rise to some uncertainty. However, already in 1995 Abram Chayes and Antonia Handler-Chayes postulated a new idea of "sovereignty": Sovereignty does not mean independence any more, but the ability of states to participate in the international community. This marked a shift in international legal thinking, and the fact that it was formulated by American authors demonstrated that the discussion did not go along the Europe vs. America line of argument.

Glennon first responded to the issue of his theoretical underpinnings raised by *Ruffert*. He agreed that he presented a Hobbesian model and therefore completely disagreed with the suggestion that compliance and not consent should qualify a rule as a norm of international law. In the viewpoint of the speaker, there are no universal values. There is no such thing as a universal system of norms in international law. He emphasized that the methodology of Kant's categorical imperative relies upon the human ability to identify what is to be universalised for purposes of determining a norm's acceptability for mankind in general. This process is inevitably subjective. Text cannot be separated from context in an objective way. A norm cannot be formulated without looking at the context of behaviour it was formulated for. The behaviour cannot be qualified without an objective referent by which the extent to which it is generalized or particularized can be determined. According to *Glennon*, there is no such objective referent. Then, the methodology of the Kantian thinking fails. He affirmed that he rejects the Kantian way of thinking.

Glennon then turned to *Thürer*'s remark that he had not given sufficient weight to the rule in international law that requires explicit renunciation of a norm. Referring to the observation by *Thürer* and others that justifying a breach of a legal norm in legal terms does in fact strengthen the norm, as the International Court of Justice (ICJ) has argued in the Nicaragua decision, he responded firstly that this argument does not amount to a rule which the U.S. had ever subscribed to. Secondly, this rule would be an unrealistic and bad one. Thirdly, not even the ICJ itself had adhered to this rule, citing the North Sea Continental Shelf case. In that case, according to *Glennon*'s reading, the court had argued that one could infer *opinio iuris* from practice. Acts do have a probative weight greater than words. On the other hand, the absence of appeal to exceptions or justifications contained in a rule does not mean that the rule is not accepted. A state can have various reasons for not appealing to a justification. Hence, one cannot demand that a state needs to appeal to justifications in order not to challenge the norm. Likewise, one cannot demand that a state explicitly renounces a rule. A state may remain silent and may not challenge a norm for various reasons, e.g. to avoid confrontation, which represents a very common motivation of state behaviour.

He then referred to instances of explicit renunciation of the rule by the U.S. On Security Council Resolution No. 1441, he cited President Bush's words after the adoption of the Security Council resolution: the U.S. had agreed to resolution 1441 but at the same time rejected to limit America's freedom of action to defend the country. As Secretary of State Colin Powell had pointed out several times the U.S. would disarm Saddam Hussein with or without the United Nations authorization. *Glennon* argued that these statements had the quality of an explicit renunciation. And looking at American diplomatic history this was not the first case of calling into question the monopoly of the UN Security Council to decide on use of force. Even President Kennedy who could be seen as a proponent of the respect of international law, underlined the' freedom of action of the U.S. in the Cuban missile crisis of 1962. The compatibility with rules of international law is not determinative for U.S. foreign policy.

The new National Security Strategy states that the U.S. will use force even in the absence of an armed attack or the imminent threat of an armed attack. No more evidence of an explicit renunciation could be asked for, anything else was splitting hairs. *Glennon* regards the standards set by the ICJ in the Nicaragua case as unrealistic standards.

Maull did not agree with *Buteux* that people felt secure nowadays. People in rich countries would not feel secure anymore after the attacks of September 11th. This feeling was supported by the chief scientific advisor to the British government showing that there was a 90 percent probability that within the next 20 years there will be a major catastrophe involving at least 1 million people killed – it could be a terrorist attack, a natural catastrophe etc. *Maull* shared this feeling of insecurity and the problem to locate its source.

In *Maull*'s opinion the challenge of global governance was that there was a fair probability that things might happen which are in nobody's interest. As an example he gave North Korea's nuclear weapons program. He questioned that this strategy was in North Korea's interest as it was an almost suicidal strategy. So the question of *Buteux* as to who benefits is not always easy to answer.

The term of "collective security", was a misnomer *Maull* continued. This concept was no longer entirely relevant because collective security was build on the assumption of the nation-state world. It referred only to relations between states. The international community had moved on, coining concepts like "cooperative security" or more recently "human security". Looking at international peace keeping efforts in the Balkans, for instance, one would see the concept of "human security" as a combination of inter-state security and nation building. This had proven to be reasonably successful in the Balkans.

Furthermore, *Maull* mentioned the implementation of international order and norms. He was concerned about whether policies work or not, not whether he liked them: with regard to American foreign policy he has found that issues in the interest of the U.S. were also in the interest of many other parties including the Europeans. There was no alternative to the U.S. playing the pivotal role in global governance. Therefore he was profoundly interested in a good American foreign policy. This interest of his, however, was unlikely to be satisfied by the current American administration, whose foreign policy was very doubtful to succeed both in the American interests and those of others. Deficient policies and structures like these would not create the desired results, such as international security. In order to solve this problem, the three forms of coordinating human behaviour should be bound together: (1) the authority of the law including the enforcement of laws, (2) the belief in ideas and norms and voluntary association, where NGOs were crucial, though one could not rely on them alone, and (3) material self interest (i.e. market mechanism). The combination of these three factors was the challenge of global governance which has not succeeded yet and was still far from succeeding, *Maull* concluded.

Professor Dr. Meinhard *Schröder* (Trier) remarked that *Oeter* might be right describing the danger of Europeans relying on the legalistic side of the international system. On the other hand, *Glennon*'s approach of unilateral renunciation of a norm has seemed difficult to follow in practice.

Secondly, he disagreed with *Langenfeld*'s remark, claiming that the U.S. was not looking for a legal basis. In fact, he had turned to the problem of how the situation would be in the future, instead of looking back to the Iraq crisis and its legality. In the case of terrorism, for example, it should rather be discussed whether pre-emptive action was possible or not.

Thirdly, *Schröder* agreed with *Dicke* on the issue of enforcement of international norms. There were international norms, like national norms, where one could say these norms were enforced or, at least, should be enforced. But there were also international norms which were observed not by enforcement, but by economic means, by persuasion.

Then Professor Dr. El-Shagi *El-Shagi* (Trier) joined the discussion, asking *Glennon* what he meant by arguing that the U.S. were building up a superior military infrastructure and thus spending an enormous amount of money for the benefit of the international community. He asked whether *Glennon* thought that the policy of the U.S. did reflect the interest of the international community or whether the U.S. even defined the interest of the international community. Moreover, *El-Shagi*, showed his surprise that, at times, the U.S. considered the UN as irrelevant as a diet club, as *Glennon* had argued; on the other hand, the U.S. position was often explained and justified by their attempt to fulfil the UN rules. In addition, he argued that the achievement of the Iraq invasion created a new field of action for Osama bin Laden and Al-Quaeda, rather than of more security.

Mr. Olivier *Frémond* (Washington) added to *Maull's* remarks on the nation state that today the nation states did not control their currency or interest rates anymore. Therefore, they were not able to control their spending. Even information was not controlled by the nation state anymore, which had been helpful to create a homogeneous culture. As a difference to the Napoleonic nation state the population was no longer culturally homogeneous. That made it difficult to fulfil the nation state's paradigm, e.g. enhancing the welfare of all its citizens. But it could enhance the opportunities for the citizens to improve their situation on their own. For instance, in the context of the global village, the nation state was no longer able to control its environment. Instead it was the state's duty to make use of its monopoly of coercion and protect its citizens from external aggression. Therefore, the U.S. population supported preemptive action overthrowing the Iraqi government, a government that provided the infrastructure for terrorism (smoking gun theory).

Professor Dr. Bernd *von Hoffmann* (Trier), remarked that *Glennon* had actually not confined himself to purely descriptive statements as he had drawn normative conclusions from description. Relating to the reasons of the failure of the UN, *von Hoffmann* highlighted the lack of power of enforcement. He suggested a change in attitudes. *Von Hoffmann* admitted that the attitude of the Europeans to constantly cut their military budgets was selfish. They had no reason to complain about American hegemony, as long as they did not fulfil their own international obligations. A change of the budgets in European countries, especially in Germany, could make a standing army of the UN possible. Now, however, the U.S. did the job the Europeans were supposed to do. The U.S. was needed dramatically: especially in the Kosovo case this had been very notable. As far as the system of the security council was concerned, *von Hoffman* raised the question whether there should only be military intervention if there was an agreement on fundamental rights and values. In his opinion, this interdependence was favourable.

Besides, *Maull* made clear that the notion of the U.S. as a hyper-power was quite misleading. The problem of international relations was not the concentration of power in the hands of the U.S. government, but the diffusion of power. He was much more impressed by what the U.S. could not do, rather than by its military power that would be pre-eminent for the next few decades.

Therefore, there was no alternative to moving to this structure of global governance to pool sufficient resources. The U.S. could not do it alone.

In the past the U.S. had recognized that. 10 years ago, in 1993, it took considerable effort to persuade the Americans to get involved in Bosnia, to overcome their unilateralism, which finally proved to be a successful mission. The situation in Rwanda was similar, where the U.S. could have applied lessons learnt in Somalia. Stationing 2000-3000 soldiers at a time, could have prevented several hundreds of thousands people killed.

Maull then turned to the Kantian paradigm. In his view, it is possible to get a broad international agreement on certain norms, e.g. the example of human rights. He admitted, that, of course, there were many regimes that did not like human rights. If, however, one questioned people in China, Indonesia or North Korea, one would often find a great deal of support for the western notions of human rights. A lot of progression hade been made recently, involving the NGOs and western governments.

As far as American doctrine of pre-emptive strikes was concerned it should be mentioned that it was not the behaviour of the U.S. government itself that caused surprise, but rather the explicitness of its mentioning in the National Security Strategy. However, because of the practical difficulties, i.e. casualties, cost and uncertainties, pre-emption would probably not become an important pattern in international relations. Instead, policy efforts would be concentrated on prevention.

Glennon agreed with *Maull* that there were limits to American power and that because of deficiencies of American power the international community was often disadvantaged. The problem of North Korea would not be resolved by pre-emptive force.

As far as his earlier statistics were concerned, which had been criticized by *Oeter*, *Glennon* made it clear that it was difficult to distinguish intra-state from inter-state conflicts. The definition in the UN Charter only applied to inter-state conflicts. His statistical figures (around 200 conflicts since 1945) were drawn from Tom Franks of New York University.

Subsequently, *Glennon* referred to the remarks of *Langenfeld* on *ius cogens* and torture. According to Amnesty International, in over 120 states state-sponsored torture had occurred. In over 80 states torture had even occurred regularly, as a matter of state policy. Therefore, the question was asked what provocative effect this had. He did not believe in *ius cogens* as a concept. If the international system was indeed consent-based, states had the power to change a norm through the development of a custom, notwithstanding the fact that the custom did not meet the criteria of *ius cogens*. In any event, the U.S.

had never accepted the principle of *ius cogens* to be part of customary international law. Moreover, one had to be realistic that even idealistic ideas would not work without the support of power, as recently seen in the case of the UN.

Referring to *von Hoffmann* he agreed that the regime governing the use of force collapsed. He concluded that the goal should be to subject the use of force to the rule of law again one day.

II. ACTORS OF GLOBALISATION

KLAUS DICKE

THE UNITED NATIONS AS AN ACTOR OF GLOBALIZATION

I. Introduction

"Excellencies, you are the United Nations. The staff who were killed and injured in the attack on our Baghdad headquarters were your staff. You had given them a mandate to assist the suffering Iraqi people, and to help Iraq recover their sovereignty."[1] This quote taken from *Kofi Annan's* address to the 58th General Assembly reveals a certain ambiguity concerning the United Nations as a political actor. On the one hand, *Annan's* address was indeed an instance of political leadership and as such qualified the deliverance of this address as a political action. On the other hand, however, *Annan's* appeal to the delegates of the United Nations member states gave evidence that political action by the United Nations depends on the political will of States. "In future," *Annan* continued, "we must take more effective measures to protect the security of our staff. I count on your full support – legal, political and financial."[2]

In order to analyze the political role of the United Nations as an actor of globalization, this paper will start by making some general observations on the legal and the political aspects of actions taken by the UN (II). The second chapter will analyze the perception of what is called "globalization" by the UN and by the UN's principal organs (III). In a third chapter I will go into the details of some of the Secretary-General's and the Security Council's answers to challenges of globalization (IV), and my concluding remarks (V) will address the question of whether or not globalization calls for reform of the United Nations.

II. The UN as an Actor – Legally and Politically

The Charter of the United Nations established an "international organization to be known as the United Nations".[3] In doing so, the originally 55 and now 191 states which ratified the UN Charter gave birth to a universal international organization which they empowered to fulfill certain political functions as de-

1 UN Doc. SG/SM/8891 of 23 September 2003.
2 Ibid.
3 Charter of the United Nations, Preamble.

scribed by the Charter. Under international law, this international organization – which meanwhile became well known as the United Nations – enjoys legal personality although its personality is to be qualified as second-class. Even modern international law[4] distinguishes between States as its "born" subjects and other bodies as elected or derived legal subjects. Despite this difference, however, it is well established since the International Court of Justice's opinion in the case "Reparation for Injuries" of 1949 that, within the boundaries of its chartered functions, the UN enjoys the international legal status of a subject of international law.

As a consequence, the UN can legally act only within the realm of explicitly ascribed powers, which States are prepared to vest in it. And the history of the UN is full of instances in which member states refused to allow the UN to act beyond this borderline.[5] Until today, to give but one example, the Secretary-General of the UN is not allowed by member States to request an advisory opinion by the International Court of Justice although this power, if exercised cautiously, would significantly enhance the Secretary-General's options to peacefully settle disputes between States, which in turn is one of the most important general functions the Secretary-General is vested with.[6] Knowledge of history, but certainly not of logic is required to understand the legal status of the UN as an international organization – at least in this regard.

On the other hand, the UN would not have persisted for 58 years, if second-class legal subjects could not act in a first-rate manner politically. And the UN certainly did so. It is sufficient to mention the Universal Declaration of Human Rights which opened the UN success story of human rights protection, the release of American pilots from Chinese prisons by Secretary-General *Dag Hammarskjold*, the General Assembly's policy of decolonization which, starting with the famous resolution "Granting of Independence to Colonial Countries and Peoples"[7], more or less peacefully directed the process of integrating former colonies which gained statehood into the international community or

4 For the legal status of international organizations under international law see *Dahm, G./Delbrück, J./Wolfrum, R.*, Völkerrecht, vol. I/2, 2nd ed., Berlin 2002, para. 105 seq.

5 One of the best known cases in point is the withdrawel of Egypt's agreement to UNEF in 1967. See *Fröhlich, M.*, Dag Hammarskjöld und die Vereinten Nationen, Die politische Ethik des UNO-Generalsekretärs, Paderborn u.a. 2002, 305.

6 Cf. *Dicke, K.*, Reformen des Sekretariats und die veränderte Rolle des Generalsekretärs, in: *Hüfner, K.* (ed.), Die Reform der Vereinten Nationen. Die Weltorganisation zwischen Krise und Erneuerung, Opladen 1994, 225-239 (234-236).

7 GA Res. 1541 (XV) of 15 December 1960.

the Conference on the Law of the Sea which eventually produced the most important global regulation in the last two decades of the 20th century. But the question remains still unanswered: What exactly did the UN do when acting in those and other instances?

At first sight, the types of action as envisaged by the Charter seem to be quite modest and reluctant: the General Assembly[8] may "discuss" or "consider", shall initiate studies and make recommendations. It has to approve the organization's budget, adopts its own rules of procedure, may request advisory opinions by the International Court of Justice, and, upon recommendation by the Security Council, appoints the Secretary-General. In cooperation with ECOSOC, it may initiate negotiations and under the provisions of the international trusteeship system it may accept petitions, provide for periodic visits and "takes these and other actions" (Art. 87). The actions to be taken by the Secretary General is framed in even more modest terms: he is to "perform" functions and duties as entrusted to him by other main organs. Only in the case of the Security Council, the Charter turns to hard-power language: Art. 24 aims at ensuring "prompt and effective action by the United Nations" and, for this purpose, vests the Council with the primary responsibility for the maintenance of international peace and security. The Council determines, decides to use forceand takes measures.

From a political scientist's point of view, this remarkably broad list of actions to be taken by the UN has to be checked against both its acceptance by member states and its practical relevance in terms of its output and its impact alike. In applying these criteria to the history of the United Nations, one can distinguish four different types of political action taken by the UN: the first is agenda setting, recommendation and policy promotion. The early history of the UN's human rights policy is the most prominent and most successful case in point. The second type is technical assistance[9] in all its aspects from planning through financing up to operational activities by, e.g., UNDP in cooperation with executive agencies like the WHO or FAO. Technical assistance is the more effective the less politicized its planning is. The third type of UN action is initiating and providing fora for negotiations in particular for multilateral treaty making. And the forth type is peacekeeping, peacemaking and peace building – from decisions by the Security Council to the preparation, organization and implementation of operations under the mandated authority of the Secretary-General.

---

8 *Tomuschat, C.*, General Assembly, in: *Wolfrum, R.* (ed.), United Nations: Law, Policies and Practice, München/Dordrecht 1995, vol. 1, 548-557.

9 *Stoll, P. T.*, Technical Assistance, in: *Wolfrum* (note 8), vol. 2, 1209-1219.

In my view, it is important to consider this whole range of actions by the UN when evaluating its actorship under the challenges of globalization because it displays a broad spectrum of working routines while at the same time revealing several constraints of actions by the UN. As, e.g., the development and application of the so-called consensus procedure shows, it is not representation but participation and negotiated consent that govern decision-making and the overall functioning of the UN system. The Security Council, however, acts on behalf of member states, i.e. on the basis of representation. As we know from the founding history of the UN and as the most recent practice of the Council has made visible once more, this specific kind of action requires legitimacy. The organization of consensus and the strife for legitimacy are the most important pre-conditions of all for UN action. Is there any change in consensus and in legitimacy brought up by the new challenges summarized under the term "globalization"?

III. Globalization and its Perception by the UN

The foundation and evolution of the UN as a political actor was the result of the economic and political process of internationalization. In contradistinction to internationalization, globalization[10] is defined as a process of denationalization which in the last two decades led to at least four developments which significantly changed the political environment in which states and the UN act: the first signs of globalization are global policies and global structures. Climatic change, the ozone layer or proliferation of weapons of mass destruction on the one hand and markets or the Internet on the other hand are examples. They have in common that they constitute political challenges beyond borders and that national and/or regional regulations fail to meet them: they call for and they enable global action. Second, globalization brings new actors on the scene: transnational corporations, non-governmental organizations, the media, and to some degree the individual, too, if one takes the indi-

10 For a broader discussion of globalization, see *Delbrück, J.*, The Globalization of Law, Politics and Markets – Implications for Domestic Law. An European Perspective, in: Indiana Journal of Global Legal Studies 1 (1993), 9-36; *Dicke, K.*, Erscheinungsformen und Wirkungen von Globalisierung in Struktur und Recht des internationalen Systems auf universaler und regionaler Ebene sowie gegenläufige Renationalisierungstendenzen, in: Völkerrecht und Internationales Privatrecht in einem sich globalisierenden internationalen System (Berichte der Deutschen Gesellschaft für Völkerrecht 39), Heidelberg 2000, 13-44 (English summary 42-44); *Teusch, U.*, Die Staatengesellschaft im Globalisierungsprozeß. Wege zu einer antizipatorischen Politik, Opladen 2003.

vidualization of responsibilities under the International Criminal Courts as an example. Third, new policy clusters emerge under the conditions of globalization: while in a cluster of internationalization non-cooperation is unfriendly but in most cases not decisive, defection becomes one of the main problems of globalization. And fourth, globalization puts forth so-called multi-level governance: regionalization is an increasing pattern of globalization as well as the integration of sub-regional, national and regional politics and the increase of corporatistic and concordant policy clusters.

It is obvious, that the UN as the only existing general and universal international organization immediately comes into the picture when political problems of globalization are at stake. But against the background of what was said in Chapter II, it is obvious, too, that the principal problems caused by globalization at the same time are principal problems of the UN. This is true in particular when it comes to the problem of non-cooperation or defection. Therefore, it is not by surprise that the perception of globalization by the UN was quite cautious: yes, globalization opens a new agenda for the United Nations, but yes, globalization bears perils and dangers, not to the least for the World Organization itself. It was a two-track answer which Secretary-General Annan put forth in numerous statements, reports and speeches.[11] As we will see later, his two-track argument resulted, *inter alia*, in the 1999 Global Compact initiative and in his latest call for reform of the United Nations before the 58th General Assembly.

In the 1990s, several organs and sub-organs of the UN started to deal with globalization on different levels and by enacting different types of activities. There were studies by the Secretariat, by UNDP and others, and in particular subjects like global governance, global commons and global markets trickled down into the UN system. The emerging activities of WTO as well as world conferences in the last decade – and the only world conference to be held in 2003 on the global information society – have put issues of globalization into the forefront of the UN's activities. In the 1990s, multilateral treaties came into being which were initiated by NGOs. The Agenda of the 58th General Assembly[12] shows at least ten topics which are directly related to globalization: "Globalization and Interdependence", "Protection of World Climate", "International Finance and Development"; "Measures to prohibit the acquisition of weapons of mass destruction by terrorists" or "Global Partnerships", to name but a few. As a closer look into the substance of those topics reveals, the UN

11 For a selection, see *Annan, K.*, Die Vereinten Nationen im 21. Jahrhundert. Reden und Beiträge 1997 – 2003, hrsg. von *Fröhlich, M.*, Wiesbaden 2004.

12 UN Doc. A/58/150.

is in the process to re-invent itself as a global actor by enacting at least the agenda-setting and promotional patterns of action as mentioned above in those fields which in the last analysis call either for enlarged patterns of cooperation or for nothing less than international legislation.[13] But is the UN really moving into the direction of a global legislator?

IV. The "Global Compact" and Acts of Global "Legislation" by the Security Council

In order to analyze how the UN reacts to challenges of globalization and which consequences and risks those reactions bear, a closer look at the details of such reactions is called for. I will refer to the example of the Global Compact initiative as launched by Secretary-General *Annan* at the Davos World Economic Summit in 1999 and three resolutions by the Security Council which indeed touch upon international legislation.

1. Global compact

With the Global Compact initiative[14] *Kofi Annan* wanted to enhance corporate social responsibility by obligating multinational corporations to international legal standards in the fields of human rights, labor law and environment protection. Companies signing the compact are allowed to make use of the Compact's logo and to present themselves as partners of the UN in their PR and business. Until May 2003, 859 (according to UN sources more than 1.000)[15] companies accepted the Compact and engaged to implement the Compact's nine principles. In three and a half years, the compact developed a structure

---

13 For an earlier evaluation of international legislation see *Dicke, K.*, Völkerrechtspolitik und internationale Rechtsetzung. Grundlagen, Verfahren, Entwicklungstendenzen, in: Zeitschrift für Gesetzgebung 3 (1988), 193-224. More recently *id.*, National Interest vs. the Interest of the International Community. A Critical Review of Recent UN Security Council Practice, in: *Delbrück, J.* (ed.), New Trends in International Lawmaking. International 'Legislation' in the Public Interest, Berlin 1997, 145-169; *id.*, Globales Recht ohne Weltherrschaft. Der Sicherheitsrat der Vereinten Nationen als Welt-Gesetzgeber?, Jena 2002.

14 *Von Schorlemer, S.*, Der "Global Compact" der Vereinten Nationen – ein Faust'scher Pakt mit der Wirtschaftswelt?, in: *id.* (ed.), Praxishandbuch UNO. Die Vereinten Nationen im Lichte globaler Herausforderungen, Berlin/Heidelberg/New York 2003, 507-552.

15 *Von Schorlemer, S.*, Multis in der Pflicht. Der Globale Pakt der UN auf dem Prüfstand, in: Internationale Politik 7/2003, 45-52 (45); United Nations, The Global Compact. Report on Progress and Activities 2002 – 2003, New York 2003, 1.

consisting of an office at UN headquarters, participation by five major UN agencies, a 20 member Advisory Council, Annual Learning Meetings, Policy Dialogues, an increasing number of domestic compacts, so-called "supply-chain initiatives" and a reporting system. NGOs are an integral part of the structure; they particularly engage in monitoring the Compact's implementation and impact. The UN describes the Compact as "an experiment in the possibilities of multi-stakeholder cooperation and collective problem solving". Its logic of action is not institution-building but networking, and consequently the UN's executive head of the Compact observed that "at the institutional level, the question is whether the United Nations as a hierarchical and bureaucratic entity is capable of sustaining the creative and entrepreneurial space that the Global Compact requires to grow".[16] The Compact idea, however, seems to have taken root within the UN system: in the context of the 2003 summit on the information society the call for a "Global Digital Compact" emerged as one of the bench marks in trying to organize such a diverse topic with its multitude of stakeholders.[17]

The growth and success of the Compact will depend on how its network will solve four main problems: first, reliable monitoring procedures on the implementation of the Compact's tasks must be established. There is growing concern among NGOs on so-called blue-washing abuses of the Compact. Second, it will be necessary to develop mechanisms to measure the Compact's impact on World Economy, on sustainability and ameliorations of social life. Third, the Compact is far from having reached common ground for its quite heterogeneous participants in their mutual understanding, their aims and purposes and their commitment to the Compact's principles. And fourth, the Compact rests on quite ambitious expectations by all participants. It will, to give but one example, be quite difficult to reconcile the compact's principle of corporate social responsibility with the principle of corporate social accountability on which, as *Sabine von Schorlemer* recently emphasized, the UN Commission on human rights is relying in its "Draft Norm on Responsibilities of Transnational Corporation and Other Business Enterprises with Regard to Human Rights".[18] Companies participating in the Compact will perhaps not be pleased by this latter approach.

16 United Nations, ibid., 2.

17 See www.gipfelthemen.de.

18 *Von Schorlemer* (note 15).

2. *Security council resolutions*

A second instance of UN reactions to globalization-induced challenges can be identified in the widening of activities by the Security Council. It is well-known that after 1990 the Council not only dramatically increased its activities but at the same time widened its understanding of "threats to the peace" according to Article 39 of the Charter.[19] In several cases the Council had to deal with typical problems of globalization and in deciding upon them it step by step came near to the field of international legislation.

The first step was the establishment of the Criminal Tribunal for former Yugoslavia by Res. 808 and 827 ten years ago. The Council followed the Secretary General's legal argument that the regular procedure to establish such a court would be multilateral treaty-making, that, on the other hand, this procedure would cause a great loss in time in the given case, and that, additionally, it would be uncertain whether all states concerned would ratify such a treaty. Therefore, the Secretary-General recommended the establishment of the Court by a resolution of the Security Council under Chapter VII. In following this recommendation the Council ruled out defection and thus met a first challenge of globalization as identified in the second chapter of the present paper. And as the reaction by *Graefrath* (who held the resolution illegal because it established an *ultra vires* act by the Council in violation of state sovereignty) revealed, this resolution raised the question of the Council's legitimacy as an international legislator.

A second challenge of globalization the Council had to face were the so-called "conflict diamonds".[20] With regard to this challenge we can observe a completely different cluster of UN action, a combination of Security Council regulations as in particular in the Sierra Leone and the Liberia cases but also with regard to Angola and, on the other hand, the so-called "Kimberley process". In quite a short period of time this process under the cooperative participation by states, the diamond industry, NGOs and the UN succeeded in introducing a certification scheme, which is based on industry self-regulation and will be implemented and monitored by means, which are established by a multilateral treaty. In this instance, the Council did not legislate *stricto sensu* although the effects of its resolutions dealing with conflict diamonds can be compared to

19 For the following, see my "National Interest" and "Globales Recht" (note 13) with further references.

20 For detailed information, see *International Peace Academy* (ed.), Economic Agendas in Armed Conflict: Defining and Developing the Role of the UN, New York 2002.

the effects of judgments by the German constitutional court ordering the federal legislator to become active.

The third and perhaps most challenging topic of globalization the Security Council is faced with is terrorism. By SC Res. 1373 of 28 September 2001 the Council made rules established by a multilateral draft treaty, which not yet had entered into force, mandatory for all UN members. In order to dry up the financing of transnational terrorism a global rule was required, and the Council established such a global rule and, additionally, established an implementation framework. By doing so it entered the field of global legislation.

V. Conclusion

What are the conclusions from the picture as drawn so far? With regard to consensus and to consensus management, to legitimacy, and to UN reform three concluding remarks are called for:

First, international legislation by the Security Council will take place in very few exceptional cases only. But the field is open and such legislation occurs. Against the background of increased activities by the Council in opening this field, increased requirements of legitimacy need to be fulfilled by the Council and by the UN as a whole. In so far, the UN is in need of reform not only in order to improve the Security Council's representativeness; additional needs for reform as well as related recommendations can easily be identified: a revitalization of the Trusteeship Council for matters of post-conflict peace-building or the revitalization of the General Assembly as a forum to discuss challenges of globalization to name but two.

Second: as the global compact and the Kimberley process show the UN took the chance offered by globalization to reinvent itself in initiating, promoting and assisting in the organization of consensus. The future of the world organization depends on the degree to which it will succeed in combining three elements of governance which were put forth by *Hanns W. Maull* in this workshop's discussions: voluntary association, market interests and legal regulation including compliance management and law enforcement.

Third: we still are at the starting point of UN reactions to globalization. I do not expect any major UN restructuring or reform on the basis of Charter amendments in the years to come but there is ample evidence that the UN indeed is capable to reform itself by adapting to newly arising tasks. Those adaption processes need time, but the changes in the last 13 years within the UN including the development of new modes of action should help us to reinvent a political virtue which has fallen somewhat into desuetude: patience.

DISCUSSION

Professor Michael *Glennon* (Medford) started the discussion, raising the question of whether Professor Dr. Klaus *Dicke* (Jena) had suggested that the Security Council had widened its powers under Art. 39 of the Charter of the United Nations, and whether this could not serve as an argument in favour of his own thesis that practice has law-making effects: If Art. 39's limits could be changed by subsequent practice why should the limits imposed by Art. 2 (4) not also be changed by subsequent practice.

Dicke replied that there were differences between Art. 39 and Art. 2 (4) of the Charter. In his opinion, Art. 39 gives the Security Council a broad discretion to decide what is meant by the terms "aggression", "breach of the peace" and "threat to the peace". By using this discretion the Security Council does not act as a juridical, but as a political organ. Therefore, the Security Council is empowered to make political decisions exercising a broad margin of appreciation. This kind of appreciation and political mechanism was not included in Art. 2 (4) of the Charter. Chapter VII of the charter formulates a procedure to enforce Art. 2 (4). *Dicke* acknowledged that Chapter VII had certain deficits, for example the insufficient enforcement of arms control and reduction. In general, he pointed out, there is a huge difference between a rule that prohibits certain acts and a chapter that opens procedure with a political margin of appreciation. *Dicke* agreed that there were different interpretations of the term "use of force", but these interpretations are embedded in the procedures of the maintenance of collective security.

Ms. Angelika *Pohlenz* (Cologne) then referred to the Global Compact Initiative. She pointed out that there were difficulties in implementing the principles of the Global Compact Initiative. For instance no mechanism exists for its enforcement, monitoring and measurement. The contracting states were looking for partners such as companies and NGOs to help implement the provisions of the Global Compact Initiative like companies and NGOs. In *Pohlenz'* opinion it is impossible to turn the Global Compact Initiative from a voluntary implication of the companies into legal binding rules. Especially U.S. American companies would not commit themselves, fearing liability in national courts. *Pohlenz* said that many states and UN agencies did not appreciate the broadening of competences of the UN Secretary General which the Global Compact Initiative implied. In the case of human rights and environment Kofi Annan had touched upon the competences of specialized agencies. But when the General Assembly decided on the Global Compact Initiative there had been a consensus on broadening the of power of the Secretary General. In the field of human rights, she acknowledged, business initiatives had their limits. However, business was most likely to change the attitudes of the people concerned, rather than the governments.

Dicke added that the essence of initiatives like Global Compact was to demonstrate the political responsibility of private actors. This became more important as the concept of human rights being rights against the state had to be modified to face novel threats to human rights by private actors, given the existence of private warfare and problems in the field of labour law.

Professor Dr. Matthias *Ruffert* (Jena) posed a question concerning the concept of "international actors" used in the speech of *Dicke*. It seemed to him that the term "international actor" was used more in a political scientist's sense. *Ruffert* wondered if "international actors" should have legal personality in the sense of international law.

Professor Dr. Meinhard *Schröder* (Trier) asked *Dicke* to elaborate more on the procedural aspects of UN reform, and its limits given the special amendment procedure of the UN Charter.

Professor Dr. Bernd *von Hoffmann* (Trier) wondered about the difference between the concepts of internationalisation and globalisation. He understood internationalisation as rule-making where the rules need to be enforced by states. In contrast to that globalisation meant a process of rule-making that does not rely on states for their enforcement.

Dicke responded that internationalisation leads to cooperation and to the establishment of international organizations. Internationalisation was relevant on the highest level of nation-state-building and is now decreasing. Responding to *Ruffert* he said, "international actors" would gradually gain legal personality, but did not yet have it in full. It was doubtful whether NGOs would ever get original legal personality like states. Globalisation, in contrast, meant a situation where political, environmental and economic problems could not be solved by the cooperation of states, e.g. global environment issues. Solutions had to be found where no defecting participant can be allowed. A feature of globalisation is the presence of multi-layered governance clusters combining nation-states, sub-state entities, international governmental organizations, NGOs, companies and private persons.

Concerning the question of internal reform of the UN, *Dicke* explained the political problems of changing the Charter. He gave the reform of budgetary procedure as an example of a reform which did not require amendment of the Charter text. The consensus of the states is the limit for informal change in the Charter. After completing his part of internal reform, Secretary General Annan is now justified to ask member states to reform the UN. *Dicke* then went on to explain the legal requirement for reforming the Charter, but he was doubtful whether such a consensus could be reached. For informal reforms, however, he saw some possibilities. For example one could introduce regional chambers as subsidiary organs of the Security Council with the right to draft resolutions.

Professor Dr. El-Shagi *El-Shagi* (Trier) commented on the statement that regionalism could be a step towards globalisation or world economy. He quoted economists arguing that regionalism lead to protectionism. One could find many arguments to endorse the assumption that an area of integration like Europe will protect its market more intensively than states that have not joined a multi state association. *Dicke* agreed and admitted that protectionism was a side effect of regionalism. *Dicke* and *von Hoffmann* agreed that the problem of protectionism was an important part of the field of activity of the WTO and UNCTAD.

PETER EIGEN

THE ROLE OF NGOs IN GLOBAL GOVERNANCE: CONTROLLING CORRUPTION – THE EXAMPLE OF TRANSPARENCY INTERNATIONAL

At Transparency International (TI) we neither shy away from confrontation if it is necessary, nor condemn other civil society organisations for pursuing different strategies, but we distance ourselves from the violence deployed by many anti-globalisation protesters in Seattle, Prague, Göteborg and – with tragic consequences – in Genoa and, most recently, in Cancun.

I. Creating a Level Playing Field

Their actions may grab the headlines, but civil society organisations need to engage with each other, and with governments and the private sector, so that our voice is heard and taken seriously by policymakers at all levels. That is the key to our approach at TI.

It is this co-operative approach that is essential to success in tackling an issue as complex as corruption in a global marketplace where corruption had become almost the norm. Businesses found themselves in a prisoner's dilemma. Those who didn't want to bribe were at a competitive disadvantage because the back-handers paid by their competitors secured lucrative contracts. To survive, a company had to bribe.

II. Making the OECD Convention Work

The OECD Anti-Bribery Convention is a striking example of the importance of this approach. The 35 signatories to the Convention account for more than 90 per cent of foreign direct investment worldwide.

The key to securing support for the OECD Convention, which came into effect in February 1999, was the support of large companies. Twenty European companies signed a letter TI drafted to their ministers that encouraged them to sign the OECD Convention.

TI managed to bring business on our side by offering an escape route from the prisoner's dilemma in which they found themselves: if companies did not bribe, they would endanger contracts in China and Indonesia, for instance, worth billions of dollars.

Under the OECD Convention, all major competitors in the world market are legally bound to stop bribing simultaneously. For instance, French or German companies can now be charged under their home countries' laws for bribing African, Asian or Latin American officials. It is all the more important, therefore, that each country feels confident that the other signatories not only introduce the appropriate legislation to implement the Convention, but that they then effectively enforce that legislation.

A follow-up process is underway at the OECD to translate this into law and practice, and civil society organisations, led by TI, are providing input and monitoring the follow-up. In November 2002, TI chapters campaigned to ensure that their governments made up the shortfall in the budget for monitoring the enforcement of the Convention in signatory countries via a peer review process. That has met with success so far, but TI will have to continue to apply pressure to ensure that the monitoring process is adequately resourced.

Between December 2001 and March 2002, Gallup International conducted the Bribe Payers Survey, a Transparency International poll of 835 senior managers in 15 emerging market economies. Only one in five respondents knew something about the Convention. These are the managers at the frontline where bribery takes place, and the results are damning evidence that OECD governments have failed to make businesses understand the new legislation.

III. The UN Convention Against Corruption

Over the past two years, TI has been working to pressure governments to agree on a UN Convention Against Corruption. The final drafting session began on 29 September. The Convention marks an important step in strengthening international cooperation on preventing and criminalizing corruption, in particular with the breakthroughs made on mutual legal assistance in the return of assets stolen by corrupt leaders.

IV. Transparency International: A Holistic Approach

While it is of paramount importance that we build coalitions on a global level, the driving force of the coalition against corruption are the national chapters of Transparency International, supported by the TI Secretariat through collecting and sharing know-how and resources, gathering knowledge and disseminating tools, in particular supporting national chapters in the evaluation and strengthening of National Integrity Systems.

TI takes a holistic approach to corruption, recognising that society has many tools to protect itself, to maintain its integrity. These include, for example: criminal law; the freedom of the press; the disclosure of the assets and liabilities of candidates for government; the independence of the judiciary and other institutions.

We have developed a system to allow governments and civil society actors to go over the strengths and weaknesses of their own National Integrity Systems, an analytical framework of checks and balances, best illustrated in TI's National Integrity Source Book.

The National Integrity System was pioneered by TI, and the Transparency International Source Book has been published in 20 languages. We have used adaptation workshops for the Source Book to invite local players to get together and expand and replace the models described in the Source Book to fit the social, legal, and economic situation in each society.

V. Integrity Pacts: An Escape from the Prisoner's Dilemma

One element of the National Integrity System that deserves particular attention is public procurement. The tool developed by TI in this field, the Integrity Pact, offers an escape route from the prisoner's dilemma. Under an Integrity Pact, bidders competing for the supply of goods and services provide a binding assurance that they have not paid any bribes in order to obtain this contract. Bidders also make an undertaking that they will not pay or accept bribes in future, and pre-agreed sanctions come into force if this undertaking is breached.

Pioneered in Argentina, Integrity Pacts are now underway in Colombia, Ecuador, Italy, Mexico, Pakistan, and South Korea.

VI. Programmes of National Chapters

The work of our national chapters is a source of strength and encouragement to us throughout the anti-corruption movement.

In 2001 the Sao Paulo municipality and the World Bank Institute reached an agreement with Transparencia Brasil to launch an anti-corruption programme in the city administration. TI Brazil applied pressure on candidates in last year's Brazilian presidential elections to make a commitment to tackle corruption if elected. They are now applying pressure on President *Lula da Silva* to make good on his promises.

Meanwhile, many chapters are pooling their ideas and their resources to become even more effective. One example where TI's national chapters are learning from each other is in the field of political accountability. In Latin America there have been Visible Candidates campaigns, monitoring campaign spending, and campaign manifestos on tackling corruption.

Likewise TI-Korea organised the Voters' Movement for Evaluation of Candidates and Participation in Elections, disclosing to the electorate background information on candidates. In 2001, our chapter in Germany injected into important state elections a process of party monitoring that was inspired by the examples of chapters elsewhere. TI Delna, the national chapter in Latvia, has also introduced an election-monitoring exercise based on the Visible Candidates model.

VII. A Coalition of Mutual Learning

The strength of the TI movement is exactly this community of mutual learning and support. It is a democratic movement, which meets every year at its Annual General Meeting. TI has succeeded in putting transparency, good governance, and the fight against corruption at the centre of the agenda of the world community.

Everybody – from *James Wolfensohn* to *Kofi Annan* – is now talking about the devastating impact of corruption on development and the need to tackle the problem. *Kofi Annan* now talks of anti-corruption measures as the tenth principle of the UN Global Compact. We have to ensure that this level of awareness to the devastating effects of corruption does not fade away from public attention in the midst of the many pressing issues facing humanity today.

Tackling corruption is indispensable if sustainable solutions are to be found to global issues such as poverty, inadequate health care provision, and decent housing, and education for all. TI will continue to fight to keep the spotlight of the global community on corruption and its appalling consequences.

VIII. The Unique Role of NGOs

TI has to focus on tasks that other players cannot credibly handle. Corruption is a clear example of an issue that governments and the private sector cannot tackle effectively alone. While government lacks the global reach, business is driven by the need to turn a profit.

In this context, civil society and its organisation and institutions have to be invited to become equal partners alongside governments and the private sector in order to form a "magic triangle". Civil society may be invited to fulfil this role, but it must also work itself into this position.

DISCUSSION

Professor Dr. El-Shagi *El-Shagi* (Trier) inquired by which method corruption was measured in the corruption perception index handed out by Professor Dr. Peter *Eigen* (Berlin). He wondered whether the ranking confirmed the assumption that corruption leads to bad economic performance while the reduction of corruption improves the performance of a country. Why were countries with a very good performance such as Mexico or China considered relatively corrupt according to their place in the ranking list (rank 64 and rank 65). Was there indeed a correlation between corruption and the development of a country?

Referring to the measurement of corruption and the elaboration of the index *Eigen* explained that 17 independent surveys had been amalgamated into one ranking. The surveys were based on interrogations of the public, professionals, academics and business people from inside and outside the countries, as well as information from the World Bank or the World Economic Forum. The results of these inquiries were then transfigured into a score system ranging from 1 for very high corruption to 10 for very low corruption by mathematical methods. Every country providing at least three surveys is listed in the ranking.

Nevertheless, he conceded, a lot of people and especially states doubt the credibility of the rankings, e.g. the President of Bolivia. had sued Transparency International (TI) after losing the elections. The President of Argentina called TI "criminal" and President *Mahatir* had called TI "western hypocrites". *Eigen* considers the index a very powerful instrument, which nevertheless is just a small part of TI's work.

Concerning the correlation between corruption and status of development *Eigen* remarked that Transparency International did not undertake such research, but that economists had discovered a correlation between freedom of information legislation and a country's position on the score list. All Scandinavian countries e.g. have such legislation and are among the top ten of the ranking. Furthermore, there was a correlation between the per capita readership of newspapers as well as foreign direct investment and the country's place on the index. Regarding corruption in Germany *Eigen* stated, that there were lots of scandals nowadays, especially in the field of politics. Nevertheless Germany moved from position 20 on the index last year to position 16 this year.

Professor Dr. Daniel *Thürer* (Zürich) thanked *Eigen* for his remarks and honoured his work as a world citizen. He expressed his support for the term of "Civil Society Organization", which *Eigen* used instead of "Non Governmental Organization". He also stated, that civil society organizations were able to influence and change politics by mobilizing the masses. *Thürer* then wondered whether the principles of TI where used as an argument in national courts deciding on disputes of private law or criminal matters, and whether TI testified in national courts. Furthermore, *Thürer* asked *Eigen* to explain the OECD convention against corruption and the measures to implement the convention into OECD law. Thirdly he wanted to know whether the work of TI in some regions of the world was considered as a mission of the north, instead of a universal one.

Eigen replied that TI tried to avoid to become involved in court cases, as TI has no knowledge of individual cases. Instead TI had been invited to hearings about national systems, e.g. in front of the American Congress about money laundering in the U.S. or in front of the German Bundestag.

Referring to the OECD convention *Eigen* explained, that the 45 signatory states of the convention undertook the obligation to criminalize bribery, even if committed in a foreign country. The ratification and implementation into national law will be controlled by mutual visits of the signatory states. According to controls made by the OECD, Germany was considered to be almost free of corruption. According to TI's own investigations, however, the picture in Germany is still mixed. The signature of the German government might be attributed to business pressure.

On the allegation that TI was promoting "Northern" values, *Eigen* pointed out that TI did everything to avoid such allegations by acting through national chapters who see transparency as a national issue. It is also empirically incorrect that corruption was only a problem of "Southern" business. It is as much a problem of business in the North.

Professor Dr. Stefan *Oeter* (Hamburg) asked whether the erosion between the public and the private sector might be considered one of the phenomena of the process called globalisation and whether this erosion formed part of the background that gave to the development of Civil Society Organizations. He fears that conferring formerly public tasks to civil society blurs the border between the public and the private. In his view, the rigidity of this distinction might be one of the main problems in fighting for transparency and struggling against corruption. Especially the closed nature of the public sphere created transparency concerns.

Eigen remarked, that in states where the public sector lacks capacities, the private sector is asked to help and fulfil targets that originally belonged to the public sector. In fact this does not affect the work of TI as it chooses its targets, its friends and its enemies, irrespective of whether they are private or public.

Finally, Professor Dr. Hanns W. *Maull* (Trier) raised the question of whether civil society needed a functioning system of law as a basis of their work, and how *Eigen* would consider the relationship between civil society and the rule of law.

Eigen responded that the lack of a legal system was a serious problem for Civil Society Organizations, but one they often had to cope with. This also meant a danger to the Civil Society Organization itself, because a shot-coming in the system of law led to less protection for civilians. For *Eigen*, the rule of law is a very basic principle of TI's work.

Furthermore *Maull* asked *Eigen* to explain the relationship between NGOs and public authorities in reference to North Korea, where NGOs helped to prop up the regime by providing the population with food. Finally, *Maull* wanted to know whether there was such a thing as privatisation of security, as the states where NGOs usually act cannot provide the security of the NGO members. Therefore the NGOs would have to hire security including weapons.

According to *Eigen*, TI tries not to hire security or use private security, but the position of TI on this matter is not absolutely clear and is to be reconsidered in the future.

ANGELIKA POHLENZ

INTERNATIONAL BUSINESS NEEDS INTERNATIONAL RULES

Already in the beginning of the 20th century business leaders from several countries convened to discuss how to jointly improve free trade and foster market economy. This led in the end to the foundation of the International Chamber of Commerce in 1919. The goal of this foundation was to get technical improvement, legal harmonization, administrative facilitation and practical help for businesses round the world. At that time the improvement of international telephone communication and the founding of an international court of arbitration were the main issues. But facilitation of customs services or harmonization of banking instruments were equally important topics.

This shows that business has for a long time been interested in internationally applicable rules, be it self-regulating or governmentally based rules. At that time the focus was laid specially on technical and practical rules working in a self-regulating way.

Since then the world has changed dramatically, but business still needs feasible rules put into action globally so as to facilitate and improve trade as well as investment, which comes along with trade in most economies nowadays.

Today, many companies and a number of economies all over the world are going through a difficult period which in some instances has turned into a crisis. Business has a clear responsibility today. Our long-term policy must be maintained. Industry is defining its own new structures as part of that process of looking to the future. ICC is responding with initiatives of its own. It is engaged in intense discussion with intergovernmental organisations about the framework in which business can operate in the future to raise living standards worldwide and to create jobs. Priorities have to be built around the basic principles, international strategies and mechanisms that are needed to respond effectively to a challenge that is becoming increasingly global.

The free flow of goods and services, investment, know-how, technology and information remains a priority for world business. Deregulation and improvement of market access must continue as a gradual process with clear objectives and take into account social costs; it must be accelerated where discriminatory double standards are still being used to defend entrenched interests. Ultimately, this process of liberalization fosters competitiveness and prosperity as the most reliable basis for individual freedom and dignity.

Freedom can only work within rules, and the same holds good for markets. Business needs the backing of effective laws, rules and institutions for its own operations and to ensure overall civil stability. Governments and intergovernmental organisations are the main rule-setters. In the last decade, governments in both industrialized and emerging economies have contributed to significant improvements. In the emerging economies, they have modernized rules of special significance to business, such as those governing stock exchanges, and have improved the protection of physical assets, equity investments, and intellectual property. On the international level, governments have completed new WTO agreements on basic telecommunications and cross-border financial services.

In this process of modernization and globalisation of rules, ICC is making a positive contribution, both as an advisor and through its own standard setting. ICC is giving a lead in the areas of trade facilitation and electronic commerce, including digital certification. New rules of arbitration, designed to meet today's more complex business environment, are in place – as are rules to combat corruption.

Broader efforts should now follow in order to foster rules-based freedom for business, with the WTO assuming a key role. Especially today, we must demonstrate the resolve to move ahead in terms of implementation and comprehensive negotiation. New negotiations to further liberalize world trade are scheduled and take place in the Post Doha Round – just showing how difficult such negotiations are in Cancun, Mexico. Business needs them to be extended to become more comprehensive than currently underway; and they should be brought to a successful conclusion without the damaging delays that characterized the Uruguay Round.

A truly global framework of rules for cross-border investment is needed, especially in view of the lack of progress so far at the OECD. A global market view will also require competition policies that impede neither trade nor investment. The question of labour standards should be addressed in order to strengthen consensus on basic rules. But we must do this in the appropriate forum of the ILO. Cross-border environmental problems should be resolved in a responsible way through multilateral environmental agreements and not by trade measures. The UNEP would be the appropriate body to deal with this. Policy-makers should be aware that truly global problems cannot be solved by isolated national or regional efforts. Being responsible and aware of these matters also means focusing on essentials and refusing to be swayed by emotional and irrational arguments.

We need this understanding to underpin agreement on basic economic goals in industrialized countries, to overcome pitfalls in emerging economies, and, ultimately, to ensure coherence of policies worldwide. Two aspects are worth highlighting:

First: The opening and deregulation of markets and the modernization and globalisation of rules and institutions relevant to business should no longer be seen as concessions to foreign investors. A truly global framework for investment is a win-win proposition. Multinationals have a well-proven record of improving social and environmental conditions in countries where they invest. In the recent Asian crisis, their long-term vision and commitment had a significantly stabilizing impact. Also, scraping non-tariff barriers is not primarily a concession to competitive emerging economies. All these actions remove stumbling blocks impeding both local and international business; they increase competition and wealth in an economy as it opens up. New international devices for continuous regulatory reform in a market perspective (such as public policy benchmarking) should now be considered. This will also help the local economy.

Second: In the new context of global markets, practical business tools such as marketing, advertising, or new financial instruments have become even more important for creating wealth in an economy. Their potential still needs to be better understood by public policy-makers.

Now, the world is shifting into a global knowledge economy – a challenge to countries and companies alike. The main contributions of business are research and innovation, the free flow of knowledge and an atmosphere of learning and re-learning. Knowledge is actively managed as an asset exposed to competition. More research and innovation, together with unprecedented growth in flows of technology, people and ideas, have become key drivers of prosperity. International firms have turned into highways and nodes in global networks for transmitting knowledge and advancing research and technology in a global perspective.

The knowledge economy needs a different framework. In recent years, developing countries have facilitated the creation and flow of technology and ideas through better enforcement of intellectual property rights. This deserves further encouragement. One big task ahead is to clarify business requirements for protecting intellectual property in the digital environment. Another is to speak up in the public debate, responding to increasing hostility towards technological progress – for instance in the field of biotechnology – in high-cost industrialized countries, and particularly in Europe.

Globalisation is not returnable and has started in the field of trade well before Marco Polo set out to conquer China. It is the only way to ensure the participation of all countries in the world in growth and wealth. Therefore it has to be successfully managed. Some aspects may enlighten this goal:

First: Business takes popular anxieties about globalisation seriously. We are aware of the plight of the unskilled and the risk that some people will be left out. At the same time, globaphobia must be opposed by improving our understanding of globalisation and its true impact on jobs and wealth. ICC has been speaking out on the benefits of globalisation; this message needs further strengthening. We must work towards encouraging all people involved to take a realistic, positive and proactive view by demonstrating that all countries can participate in the gains from globalisation, provided that they focus on the right policies. We must confront allegations of social dumping with the reality of greater overall wealth and the rapidly increasing number of people living above the poverty line.

Second: Not everything becomes global – supply will, but not consumption. (This is the reason for the quote of business Think global, act local") The greater choice open to the consumer increases the diversity of local demand. Some critics of globalisation say that countries that integrate into world markets lose their societal and ethical values; they warn that civilizations will clash. Societal values will indeed be increasingly exposed to global competition and dialogue. But this will enrich mankind by offering choice, cross-fertilization and strengthening of ideas and values that are respected by all cultures and societies. Companies dealing abroad are aware that local values should be maintained and fostered. As companies go global, they propagate trust. Businesses oriented towards the long-term share a wider range of values than shareholder value alone.

Third: A key challenge in the context of a rules-based freedom for business is to prevent financial meltdowns and maintain a stable international financial system. We have seen the introduction of the euro being a major innovation in this system. Its arrival has not been only a matter of European politics; it raises big issues of global governance with respect to the future relationship between international currencies. It will inevitably have far-reaching policy repercussions – for instance, with regard to the US current account deficit.

Global governance and the adequacy of international organisations require priority consideration. Competencies – supranational, national, subnational and global – must be reorganized according to a broader overall view. Currently, too much duplication and inadequate coordination are preventing intergovernmental bodies from handling effectively the complex and interrelated problems of the early 21st century. Intergovernmental organisations will need additional authority, but with the proviso that they must pay closer attention to the contribution of business and competition to wealth creation, recognize the need for less bureaucracy, and bring a clear focus to really important global problems. These reforms have now started, but they are of course a long-term undertaking. Once the UN's own structure is overhauled, it and its General Secretariat would be the natural choice to assume responsibility for coordinating international decision-making more efficiently. It is in this perspective that we think that a strong UN is good for business.

A more substantive involvement of business must be part of the reform. Here, ICC has confirmed and strengthened its position as the voice of business through a close working relationship with the WTO and constructive consultations with the UN Secretary General and the heads of UN agencies. ICC is able and willing to contribute to agenda building, to substance and to a constructive follow-up. Our positioning in the dialogue reflects the key function of business – to create wealth.

There is a need to clarify leadership and to define shared responsibility, with roles for an extended G-8, the European Union and key areas of the developing world.

Globalisation creates new threats. Authorities must cooperate in the fight against new forms of organized crime threatening firms (counterfeiting, cyber crime, fraud, etc). Critical infrastructure on which communities depend – telecommunications, banking and finance, energy, transportation, government services – require protection through the joint commitment of the leading economies and the private sector.

It is the individual markets in different countries where reality takes place. Those markets benefit from stable, strong and efficient government. Though many countries in the developing world now have implemented incentives for business to attract their investment – as means to create new jobs and by this growth and in the end wealth. What is often forgotten is that investments are done for several reasons, the least important of which are incentives from governments that are neither stable nor reliable. Markets with the prospect of being sustainable, infrastructure, skilled labour force, reliable administration and a legal structure with independent courts are much more important for business than incentives which could be withdrawn if the governments wish to.

Increased reliance on markets and competition calls for governments that are able to refrain from regulation where possible, but also to set and strictly implement rules where necessary. Only stable, ordered and honest societies prosper. This also applies for the non-existence of corruption.

In countries with extensive entitlements and aging populations, we must examine the issue of long-term imbalances in the welfare state in order to take decisions to ensure the sustainability of pension schemes (which will include longer lifetime work) – and, ultimately, the state, its institutions and the trust of citizens.

ICC recognizes how societies are changing, with citizens speaking up and expressing their deep-felt concerns. However, in some respects, the emergence of activist pressure groups risks weakening the effectiveness of public rules, legitimate institutions and democratic processes. These organisations should place emphasis on legitimising themselves, improving their internal democracy, transparency and accountability. They should assume full responsibility for the consequences of their activities. Where this does not take place, rules establishing their rights and responsibilities should be considered. Business is accustomed to working with trade unions, consumer organisations and other representative groups that are responsible, credible, transparent and accountable and consequently command respect. What we question is the proliferation of activist groups that do not accept these self-disciplinary criteria.

Economic nationalism, negative-sum disputes, unilateralism and extraterritorial imposition of national laws should not be confused with strong government; they are out of step with the realities of a global economy. But nationalist reflexes keep coming back – recently, for instance, on tax issues. Countries compete against each other for a higher share of corporate taxes through closer scrutiny of so-called transfer pricing, taxation of technical assistance, etc. thereby increasing the burden on international firms – both in terms of tax rates and paperwork. In many areas of regulation, countries seek to impose their own standards instead of relying on mutual recognition.

Six conclusions can be drawn from these considerations:

1. We need to achieve a balance between freedom and rules for running a business.
2. Understanding of key market mechanisms still needs to be fostered.
3. Business and rule-setters must respond to today's most important challenge, the emergence of a global knowledge economy.
4. We must overcome a diffuse but virulent globaphobia, address the real problems that hinder wealth and job creation, and we must make globalisation a success.
5. On many issues of global concern, decision-making must now also become global, with business involved in a meaningful policy dialogue.

6. National governments will continue to have a key role in the future; economic growth and societal stability require strong and efficient governments.

Globalisation as said needs international rules so as to allow globally acting businesses to compete on a level playing field that is known and respected by all. This is the only way to guarantee fair competition and reliability for all parties concerned.

Rules can be made by business itself or have to be set and implemented by governments. As far as business is concerned we find them on national as well as international level. The International Chamber of Commerce has been set up to draft internationally used rules and still is acting on this behalf.

ICC model contracts and clauses, uniform rules and voluntary codes are elaborated after extensive consultation with business worldwide. They provide practical and efficient tools to facilitate international business transactions.

ICC model contracts give parties a neutral framework for their contractual relationships: their provisions have been drafted to ensure consistency with the parties' legal systems without expressing a bias for any one particular legal system. They are flexible and user-friendly contractual tools and are used in countless daily transactions.

ICC voluntary codes cover market and advertising, the suppression of extortion and bribery and sound environmental management practices. ICC codes are often applied as a reference point for solving national or cross-border disputes. They can be effective in three ways: they can be enacted in national legislation; they can be applied directly by companies, professional associations and self-regulatory bodies; or they can be adapted to local or specific professional requirements.

Other fields business relies on nowadays are:

Arbitration

Established in 1923 as the arbitration body of ICC, the ICC International Court of Arbitration has pioneered international commercial arbitration as it is known today. Over the decades, the Court has led the way in securing the worldwide acceptance of arbitration as the normal and most effective means of resolving international commercial disputes and in demonstrating the advantages of institutional arbitration compared with ad hoc arbitration. Further, ICC initiated and led the movement that resulted in the adoption in 1958 of the New York Convention on the Recognition and Enforcement of Foreign Arbitral Awards – the most important multilateral treaty in international arbitration.

Expertise

Founded in 1976, the ICC International Centre for Expertise offers experts with specialized knowledge to assist business in a variety of situations, such as serving as witnesses and helping resolve differences. The Centre may be called upon to propose experts, appoint experts, and administer expertise proceedings. The Centre also administers the ICC Rules for Documentary Credit Dispute Resolution Expertise (DOCDEX) and

ADR

The ICC ADR Rules enable ICC to offer a service for settling business disputes amicably, flexibly, and at minimum cost in time and money, with the help of a third party known as a neutral. The Rules allow the parties to choose whichever settlement technique they consider best suited to resolving their dispute – mediation, neutral evaluation, mini-trial, and others.

The internationally used rules cover a wide area of sectors:

Banking and Finance

Uniform Customs and Practice for Documentary Credits (UCP 500, Revised 1993), Uniform Rules for Demand Guarantees (URDG 458, 1992), and Uniform Rules for Collections (URC 522) are used daily worldwide to finance international business and are endorsed by the United Nations Commission on International Trade Law (UNCITRAL). Of these, UCP 500 are the most successful with banks all over the world incorporating them in their letters of credit. The UCP 500 have also been incorporated into many national laws including in the US and developing countries. The eUCP, a supplement to UCP 500 to deal with all-electronic and part-electronic presentations of documents under documentary credits, came into force in April 2002. The supplement is expected to be widely used as electronic documents increasingly take the place of paper-based documentary credits.

The use of the URDG 458, mentioned above, is expected to be enhanced as a result of the World Bank's decision in 2002 to incorporate these rules in its unconditional guarantee forms.

International Standby Practices (ISP98, adopted 1999) are relatively new ICC rules governing the use of standby letters of credit.

Marketing and Advertising

The ICC marketing codes are among the most successful self-regulatory instruments. The principles laid down by the codes are generally accepted and followed by business and can be found in most national and sectoral codes. Since its first edition in 1937, the ICC International Code of Advertising Practice has proven to be the undisputed model for such codes. The European Advertising Standard Alliance (EASA), through its common principles and recommendations of best practice, requires its members to adhere to the fundamental principles of the ICC International Code of Advertising Practice, reinforcing ICC's role as the reference point for global standards.

The recently revised International Code of Sales Promotion (2002) continues the well-established policy of promoting high standards of ethics in marketing by self-regulation against the background of national and international law. The code is designed primarily as an instrument for self-regulation but is also intended for use by the courts as a reference document.

Like all ICC marketing codes, the International Code of Sales Promotion aims to create a balance between the interests of business and consumers, whilst maintaining freedom of choice for business between different marketing tools.

The ICC/ESOMAR International Code of Marketing and Social Research Practice is the leading code in the field of market and social research. 4000 ESOMAR members in 100 countries apply this code daily.

Insurance

ICC Uniform Rules for Contract Bonds (URCB, 1994) were developed to regulate the provisions of conditional guarantees. Their use is increasingly widespread. From April 1997, both central and local governments in Japan generally use performance bonds under URCB. It is estimated that 101 000 contract bonds were issued during fiscal year 1997. The URCB have been endorsed by UNICTRAL, in July 2000, and by many industry associations, including the International Federation of Consulting Engineers (FIDIC), PanAmerican Surety Association (PASA), Surety Association of America (SAA), and International Credit Insurance and Surety Association (ICISA). The URCB are available in Chinese, Italian, Korean, English, French, Japanese, Spanish, Danish, Portuguese, and Icelandic. The Explanatory Guide (1997) exists in English, Spanish, Japanese, and Portuguese.

Customs

ICC Customs Guidelines were developed with the assistance of the World Customs Organization (WCO) as a set of business principles to which modern and efficient customs administrations should adhere. The substance of the guidelines has been incorporated into WCO's revised International Convention on Simplification and Harmonization of Customs Procedures adopted by the WCO Council in June 1999. In 2003 they were complemented with Explanatory Notes, which expand the bare text of each guideline and identify its advantages to government, business and customs.

Commercial Law and Practice

Incoterms 2000

Incoterms 2000 are the ICC rules for the interpretation of the 13 trade terms commonly used in international sales contracts. These terms are regularly incorporated into sales contracts worldwide and have become part of the daily language of international trade.

Incoterms 2000 make international trade easier and help traders in different countries to understand one another. Incoterms 2000 state the seller's and buyer's respective obligations in an international sale contract and are referred to by traders in countless thousands of transactions every day. First published by ICC in 1936, they have been periodically revised to take into account the latest developments in international trade such as containerisation, development of multimodal transport, and use of electronic data interchange.

Incoterms 2000 are the most widely applied version of Incoterms ever. They are constantly used in countries such as the US and China in which the use of the previous version, Incoterms 1990, was not systematic. Incoterms 2000 are available in more than 31 languages and additional translations will be released soon.

Incoterms 2000 have been endorsed by UNCITRAL. This endorsement involves the legal recognition of Incoterms 2000 and the recommendation of Incoterms 2000 to UN regional or local agencies. When drafting the United Nations Convention on Contracts for the International Sale of Goods (CISG), UNCITRAL specifically stated that the interpretation of trade terms should be left outside the scope of the convention and referred to Incoterms 2000 as the authoritative rules for the interpretation of trade terms. Incoterms 2000 have also been endorsed by the Economic Commission for Europe of the United Nations (UN/ECE) in the recommendation number 5.

ICC Model Contracts

ICC Model Commercial Agency Contract – 2nd edition (2002) provides a flexible solution to parties negotiating agency agreements abroad. Using uniform contractual rules and not based on any specific national law, the model incorporates prevailing practice in international trade as well as the principles generally recognized by the domestic laws on agency. This fully revised second edition takes into account recent developments in the laws of agency, including Internet sales.

ICC Model Distributorship Contract (Sole importer-distributor) (2002). Distributorship contracts are one of the most frequently used means of organizing the distribution of goods in a foreign country. Almost every company engaged in international trade has at least some agents abroad and so most exporters will at some stage be faced with drafting an international distributorship agreement.

The ICC Short Form Model Contracts (2001). Two of ICC's best-selling model contracts – the International Agency Contract and the International Distributorship Contract – are now available in simplified short forms. Developed and published in response to popular demand, the short forms provide the perfect working tool for those parties who are making relatively straightforward transactions and who have no need for detailed provisions. As such, they save time and costs.

ICC Model International Franchising Contract (2000) provides guidance on drafting cross-border franchise agreements and a credible alternative to model contracts elaborated by public authorities without consulting business. It strikes a fair balance between the interests of the franchiser and franchisee.

ICC Model Occasional Intermediary Contract (Non-circumvention and non-disclosure agreement) (1999) responds to the business need for a reliable and globally accepted instrument protecting the intermediary's right in an international transaction.

ICC Model Sale Contract (Manufactured goods intended for resale) (1997) has been used as a model by the International Trade Centre (a joint UNCTAD/WTO organisation) for the elaboration of the model contract and user's guide for the international commercial sale of perishable goods.

With thousands of copies sold, these clauses and rules have a considerable impact on current commercial practice all over the world.

ICC Force Majeure Clause 2003 and ICC Hardship Clause 2003 provide international traders with ready-made, off the peg model clauses which parties to international contracts may incorporate into their contracts.

ICC Force Majeure Clause 2003 combines the predictability of listed force majeure events with a general *force majeure* formula intended to encompass circumstances that fall outside the listed events.

ICC Hardship Clause 2003 balances the legitimate expectation of contract performance with the harsh reality that circumstances can change so as to make performance so difficult that a contract has to be modified.

E-Business, Information Technologies and Telecommunications

ICC Best Practices for Online Dispute Resolution Services for Business-to-Consumer and Consumer-to-Consumer Disputes (2003) provide guidance for companies and consumers engaged in online transactions, as well as for online dispute resolution service providers, to ensure effective services that consumers and companies can both count on. They focus on the specific issues raised by conducting alternative dispute resolution online, and follow the recommendations and best practices emerging from business and concerned organisations.

ICC Best Practices for Customer Redress (2003) provide guidance for companies transacting online on emerging best practice in customer redress with a view to improving consumer confidence in buying online.

ICC Handbook on Information Security Policy for Small to Medium Enterprises (SMEs) provides assistance to SMEs to help them improve the information security of their business. It offers guidance on how to develop, implement and review their own company information security policy, and to deal with important issues such as personnel and physical security, encryption and business continuity in adverse circumstances.

Model Contract for Privacy Protection in Transborder Data Flows (1992) is endorsed jointly by ICC, the Council of Europe and the European Commission. This contract has been incorporated in countless thousands of business contracts that required the cross-border transmission of personal data. ICC is currently working with other business organisations and liasing with the European Commission to develop a new model contract for trans-border data flows that would facilitate global transfers and be compliant with the 1995 European data protection directive.

ICC Uniform Rules of Conduct for Interchange of Trade Data by Teletransmission (1988) have been of fundamental support to the growth in use of Electronic Data Interchange (EDI) in all sectors of business.

ICC General Usage in Digitally Ensured Commerce (GUIDEC – 1997, GUIDEC II – 2001). These guidelines set forth what parties involved in e-signature practice can reasonably expect from each other. They have set a worldwide standard for this emerging practice, and have formed the basis of work on e-signatures in UNCITRAL, the OECD, the European Commission and others.

Transport

In 1992, ICC and UNCTAD issued the *UNCTAD/ICC Rules for Multimodal Transport Documents*. They continue to set the only globally accepted standard for multimodal transport documents. The UNCTAD/ICC Rules represent a reasonable compromise of shipper and carrier interests and work by their incorporation into private transport contracts. These rules provide a uniform legal regime for transport operations that include more than one mode. They have simplified documentation and practice and have served as a catalyst in the implementation of legislation worldwide. The Andean Community Decision 331 of March 1993 and the Indian Multimodal Transport legislation of April 1993 are both regimes that are largely based on the UNCTAD/ICC Rules. The UNCTAD/ICC Rules have also been incorporated in several widely used standard transport documents such as the FIATA Multimodal Transport Bill of Lading and the BIMCO Combidoc.

Environment

ICC Business Charter for Sustainable Development – Principles for Environmental Management. Launched in 1991, the Charter is now widely accepted as one of the foundation stones for corporate environmental management and provided a basis for the development of the UN Global Compact. The ICC promotes the Charter as a set of "good practices" comprising 16 principles for companies to endorse when establishing responsible environmental programs. Companies are not measured against the Charter as they might be measured against an industry standard or code (like ISO). Instead, the Charter advocates a progressive path to follow.

Environmental Management System Resource Training Kit is a joint initiative with the United Nations Environment Programme (UNEP) and the International Federation of Consulting Engineers (FIDIC) launched in January 1997.

The kit is available in 14 languages and has been widely disseminated through business and industry networks worldwide. It has recently been comprehensively revised and has proved its value as an excellent practical tool.

ICC Code on Environmental Advertising (1991) provided the first international industry guidance on the use of environmental issues in advertising. It is widely respected and remains relevant today.

Anti-Corruption

From their introduction as part of the 1977 ICC Report on Extortion and Bribery in business transactions, the *ICC Rules of Conduct to Combat Extortion and Bribery in International Business Transactions (revised in 1999)* have sought complementary and mutually supportive action by governments, intergovernmental bodies, and the business community to combat extortion and bribery in international trade with significant success. As a result of the rules, corporations in a number of countries have been prompted to establish or strengthen their internal rules of fair practices, taking as a model the ICC Rules of Conduct. For instance, Shell, Nestlé and ABB have made specific mention of acceptance of the ICC rules in their own corporate materials. Further success in promoting use of the ICC rules amongst businesses followed the publication in 1999 of a practical guide to the implementation of the rules and other anti-corruption initiatives. This book – Fighting Corruption: A Corporate Practices Manual – has been fully revised and updated in 2003. The ICC Rules of Conduct have also led to close cooperation with the OECD on corruption work, particularly the OECD Convention on Combating Bribery of Foreign Public Officials in International Business Transactions. The two instruments are seen as complementary, with the 1999 revision of the Rules containing a preface on the implications of the Convention and dealing with the additional problem of private-to-private sector bribery. The German National Committee has developed with the help of German business a practical guide to implement anti-corruption rules into companies. These have been adopted by a number of German companies and are used by others as a base for companies' internal codes of conduct.

Thus, ICC rules are both: just rules to be used and implemented by companies round the world itself and rules that trigger legislation in many countries as well as being used by international governmental organisation as base for their negotiation and inter-governmental agreements.

DISCUSSION

The discussion was opened by Professor Dr. Paul *Buteux* (Winnipeg) who asked what was meant by the phrase "Business requires a level playing field". He suggested that it could firstly mean that everybody was subject to the same, specific rules. In this case, however, it would be a very demanding requirement to accomplish such a level playing field. Secondly, it could be understood as non-discrimination. This would require more general rules and was not as demanding in terms of global government.

In both cases, he pointed out, the discussion about a level playing field was highly contested. As examples he cited the discussion on a multilateral agreement on investment (MAI) which created a lot of NGO opposition as well as the controversial discussion on intellectual property rights. For the latter example, it is ironical in his opinion that the United States of America, who had been the biggest pirates of intellectual property in past centuries, were now pushing the protection of intellectual property. He stated that theft of intellectual property is and has been very common and that quite a few countries make part of their business from this.

Buteux then considered that one argument that can be made against establishing the same rules for intellectual property on a global basis is that it could actually mean discrimination against developing countries. This would also t be an argument against "globalisation". Globalisation is said to be discriminatory and in fact hinders development. Although he would not agree totally with this argument, he stressed the point that the push for some form of globalisation was a product of the rich and secure, not the weak and insecure. He wondered whether a "level playing field" was not created on a global, but rather a regional basis like the EU or NAFTA.

Ms. Angelika *Pohlenz* (Cologne) replied to *Buteux*'s first question that non-discrimination would be the first step. But she went on to stress that global corporations, especially smaller ones, suffered from the multitude of national laws they are required to observe. It would reduce costs if there was a certain similarity in laws. Recalling the multilateral agreement on investment (MAI) *Buteux* had referred to, *Pohlenz* claimed that this initiative had been supported by business because it implied non-discrimination and security for investment. In her opinion, we cannot ask for the same rules in every country because countries are not alike. But demanding non-discrimination means asking for certain basic rules that need to be established in each country. This would also be what the WTO does, they agree on topics in the member countries.

Pohlenz then turned to the intellectual property rights issue. She claimed that intellectual property needed protection, otherwise investment into research would stop. The extent of the protection, however, needed to be debated.

Professor Dr. Peter *Eigen* (Berlin) then rose to speak. He expressed his dislike of the phrase "Deregulation is fighting corruption". In his opinion, this is entirely wishful thinking. He stressed that there were different kinds of regulation and that they represented a necessary instrument in order to fight corruption as well as to protect the functioning of the markets, especially in the field of anti-trust. *Eigen* claimed that there was a need for regulation allowing the positive forces of the market to function as a regulator and as an allocator, and at the same time providing for corrections wherever the outcome was not acceptable to society, politically or socially. Regulation was particularly desirable on a global scale as there is no visible hand to correct market failures Therefore governance in a globalised economy is essential. Without regulations, big businesses would have problems to operate, though they would operate better than small business. He again focused on his argument that deregulation would not mean fighting corruption but might instead create corruption.

Pohlenz replied that for her the term "deregulation" did not mean the complete abolition of rules of all kind. Deregulation in her view means getting rid of superfluous bureaucracy and does not amount to cancelling rules that are good for the welfare or the functioning of business. Too much bureaucracy, she argued, gives too much power to civil servants which can lead to corruption. This was the correlation expressed by the phrase: "Deregulation means fighting corruption".

This was visible in Europe. In her opinion, the European market does not need so much consumer protection unless the image of the consumer is that of a stupid person. She also claimed that there were too many bureaucrats in Brussels that set up all sorts of rules in order to make themselves indispensable. Finally she reiterated her worries that overruling stifles markets. She concluded that a certain amount of rules was necessary but there was a substantial danger of excessive bureaucracy.

Professor Dr. El-Shagi *El-Shagi* (Trier) agreed with *Pohlenz*. He also pointed out that deregulation did not mean no regulation at all but rather avoiding regulations unnecessary for the functioning of the market system. Regulation in the sense of protection of competition or protection of environment etc. was needed. The speakers agreed that "over-regulation" was a better term to be used.

El-Shagi then turned to the intellectual property issue. In his view, it is not correct that applying the same rules on intellectual property rights in every country means discriminating against developing countries. Any special treatment of countries means costless transfer of property rights. He could see no justification for such a policy.

Buteux stressed that by saying plenty of countries benefit from theft of intellectual property, he had not intended to indicate that this was the right way to go; it was not. He simply meant to state that even highly developed states basically advocate the theft of intellectual property. For example the Canadian government insisted that Canadian drug firms which are subsidiaries to American firms sell drugs to Africa at a particular price.

El-Shagi wanted to distinguish this from theft of intellectual property because in this case, restrictions to re-export these drugs to Canada are made and it is therefore not possible to get those drugs at a reduced price in Canada. He could not imagine a market system functioning without the protection of intellectual property rights.

III. GLOBAL DEVELOPMENT POLICY

Wolfgang Weiß

THE ROLE OF THE WTO IN GLOBAL DEVELOPMENT POLICY

I. Introduction

The WTO is an organization that administers and implements trade agreements. Under its umbrella the world trade order is shaped by multilateral negotiations on trade and trade-related issues that provide for new rules and standards. The WTO is not a development institution as it is not a centre for analysis of and research in the development needs of the poor countries or for the exchange of ideas and positions between north and south with subsequent decisions being taken on which development policy to follow. The WTO does not constitute a forum to formulate development strategies and objectives.

However, this does not mean that the WTO does not have a role to play in development policy. First of all, trade is not an end in itself. Free trade aims at gains in wealth to the benefit of all countries' development. As raising wealth is also the objective of development policy the WTO has a development dimension since the objectives basically are the same. Development policy, however, particularly focuses on the development needs of poor countries whereas reducing trade barriers is a concept working for the good of all states in an overall perspective without looking to the peculiar problems of developing states. Even in this respect the WTO is of interest to development policy since it enshrines provisions designed specifically for developing countries.

Secondly, from a practical development perspective, trade is a key element of development strategies. To many developing states trade is more important than development aid. Developing less developed countries requires an increased integration of the developing countries' economies into global trade as this leads to rising economic welfare. Economists state a correlation of open markets and economic growth. Although this does not indicate the direction of causality, analyses in their broad majority back the assumption that the opening of a market leads to gains in growth and welfare there. A new research report by the World Bank shows that in developing countries that have integrated into the world economy, globalisation has helped to reduce poverty, whilst in those that failed to do so, poverty has increased.[1] The integration of

---

1 The study Globalisation, Growth and Poverty: Building an Inclusive World Economy, 2001, by *Collier, P./Dollar, D.*, reveals that 24 developing economies that successfully integrated into the world economy in the last 20 years achieved higher

economies into global trade is covered by the mandate of the WTO[2] since it provides for increased free trade and liberalized access to international markets by restraining the barriers to cross border trade. The WTO organises concerted multilateral negotiations on tariff reductions and removal of non-tariff barriers. Furthermore, WTO rules help to integrate developing states into international markets by supporting reforms of developing countries' own policies as the WTO agreements provide a set of rules and procedures governing the trade policies of the WTO members.[3] The development relevance of the WTO in this respect is quite high all the more as about 100 of its 146 (September 2003) members are developing countries and presumably more than 90 % of world trade is done by the WTO members. On the other hand, the WTO disciplines can impede development if the implementation of rules binds resources which are needed in other areas of greater development importance.

Despite the merits of liberalized trade, there is no doubt that many developing countries have not been able to integrate into the world economy. The poorest, the least developed countries have been marginalized. Their share in global trade has declined from 0.8 percent in 1980 to 0.4 percent in 2001. To make progress in development, the poorest countries need to be drawn into the global economy and increase their access to modern knowledge and technology.

Reducing this marginalisation and promoting the development of developing countries places challenging tasks to the global trading system. Global governance in the field of development policy has to take care that the trading system also works for the poor. For this reason, improving the governance of the global trading system as regards development is a common responsibility of the international community. The proposed Millennium Round of trade negotiations was supposed to be a development round. At Doha the WTO members

growth in incomes, longer life expectancy and better schooling. They enjoyed, on average, a growth rate in income of 5 % per capita compared to 2 % in rich countries. Less globalized countries such as sub-Saharan Africa and the Middle East on average experienced a rise in poverty and negative growth rates. The report proposes an agenda for action to help the developing countries to minimize the risks and maximize the advantage of globalisation.

2 *Blackhurst, R.*, The Capacity of the WTO to Fulfil its Mandate, in: *Krueger, A.* (ed.), The WTO as an International Organization, 1998, 44-47.

3 *Finger, M./Winters, A.*, What Can the WTO do for Developing Countries?, in: *Krueger, A.* (ed.), The WTO as International Organization, 1998, 365.

finally adopted a Ministerial Declaration that is called a development agenda. At least it pretends to put the development needs at the centre of attention.

This paper analyses the development relevance of the WTO and makes some proposals to improve the development effects of the WTO. For this purpose, the next section will present the rise of the development issue in the history of GATT and WTO and look to the Doha Agenda. Then the development dimension of the rules in general and of the special and differential treatment provisions in particular will be highlighted before suggestions to increase the development dimension of the WTO can be formulated.

II. WTO's Increasing Awareness of Development Issues

1. Trade and development in GATT and WTO

a) In contrast to the Havana Charter for an International Trade Organization[4], which dedicated a whole chapter (Chapter III) to economic development, development was almost not an issue for GATT 1947. Later reforms of the GATT rules and disciplines, which were driven by development concerns, always (apart from changes of Article XVIII in 1955) were initiated by decisions and resolutions taken outside GATT. The establishment of the United Nations Conference on Trade and Development (UNCTAD) influenced the insertion of the new Chapter on Trade and Development into GATT in 1965 and was crucial for the adoption of particular GATT provisions like the Generalized System of Preferences in 1971[5] and of other later GATT development measures (the Enabling Clause of 1979[6]; the Global System of Trade Preferences among devel-

---

4 Extracts are reprinted in: International Law Quarterly, vol 2, 1948, 283.

5 See UNCTAD Res. 21 (II); *Benedek, W.*, Preferential Treatment, in: *Dicke, D./Petersmann, E.-U.* (eds.), Foreign Trade in the Present and a New International Economic Order, 1988, 80; *Jackson, J. H.*, The World Trading System, 2000, 322 et seq.; *Petersmann, E.-U.*, International Trade Order and International Trade Law, in: *Oppermann, T./Petersmann, E.-U.* (eds.), Reforming the International Economic Order, 1987, 224.

6 See the declaration on "Differential and More Favorable Treatment, Reciprocity and Fuller Participation of Developing Countries", GATT Basic Instruments and Selected Documents 26S (1980)/203. This Clause made a differential and more favorable treatment an integral part of the GATT system and provided a permanent basis for the Generalized System of Preferences. *Bhala/Kennedy*, World Trade Law, 1999, 424 et seq; *Jackson, J. H.*, The World Trading System, 2000, 323; *Yusuf, A.*, Differential and More Favourable Treatment, Journal of World Trade Law, vol.14, 1980, 488.

oping states resulting in a GATT waiver in 1989[7]). The UNCTAD conferences became the main forum for the developing countries to articulate and enforce their economic ideas whereas GATT to a large extent was content (as far as development issues were concerned) with the implementation of development commitments adopted outside. There were two reasons for that: the development issue fell outside the scope of GATT trade negotiations focusing on tariff reduction (apart from the Tokyo Round) and the developing states did not effectively participate in GATT.

The preferences granted to the developing countries (GSP, Part IV of GATT, Enabling Clause) resulted in almost no binding obligations for developed states. Furthermore there were other developments that undermined the demands of the developing countries resulting in non-tariff barriers to trade of goods in the particular interest of developing states (Multifibre Arrangement; grey area measures; agricultural sector remaining essentially outside the GATT).[8]

b) The establishment of the WTO showed some albeit minor improvements as regards the development issue being the result of improved developing states' participation in the Uruguay Round negotiations. The Punta Del Este declaration, which launched the Uruguay Round, several times mentioned the needs of the developing countries but was far away from making development the core issue of the Round. What is new in the WTO compared to GATT 1947 is that the development needs of the developing countries were mentioned as an objective of the WTO, yet in a limited form: The member states recognized in the preamble of the WTO Agreement that there is a need for efforts to ensure that developing countries and especially the least developed among them secure a share in the growth in international trade commensurate with the needs of their development. This aim was new, but far from setting the developing countries needs on the top of the agenda. Firstly, it should not be ensured that the developing countries' exports have a share in international trade, but only a share in the growth of the international trade. Secondly, this objec-

---

7 *Trebilcock, M./Howse, R.*, The Regulation of International Trade, 2nd edition 2000, 378; *Matsushita, M./Schoenbaum, T./Mavroidis, P.*, The World Trade Organization, 2003, 385.

8 See *Michalopoulos, C.*, The Role of Special and Differential Treatment for Developing Countries in GATT and the World Trade Organization, World Bank Policy Research Working Paper No. 2388, 2000, 9; *Hart, M./Dymond, B.*, Special and Differential Treatment and the Doha "Development" Round, JWT 2003, 401 et seq.

tive was far from addressing all needs of the developing countries. Thirdly, it was listed in the end of the indicative list of WTO objectives, even after protection and preservation of the environment and sustainable development. Additionally, the Marrakesh Agreement contains a Ministerial Decision on Measures in Favor of Least-Developed Countries which recognizes the difficult circumstances of these countries and gives them special treatment with regard to all aspects of all the agreements: they will only be required to undertake commitments to the extent consistent with their development needs and institutional capacities.[9] This was a consequence of the insight (at least since UNCTAD IX it became common sense) that liberalization and globalised markets do not only result in a win-win situation but that some countries, in particular the least developed countries, might continuously be marginalized. The special and differential treatment of the developing states was strengthened by the Uruguay Round agreements. They contain a lot of new differential and more favourable treatment provisions (now legally binding) increasing trade opportunities by preferential market access, calling upon WTO members to safeguard the interests of developing states when implementing the WTO agreements, granting flexibility of commitments and providing transitional periods and technical assistance. This, however, was not voluntarily done in favour of the developing states but was a consequence of the extension of the GATT to new areas and of the single undertaking rule. The developing countries did not have the capacities to implement the commitments in some of the new areas so that they would not have signed the Marrakesh agreement unless these new features were conceded to them.[10]

The way in which the needs of the developing states were stressed by the Uruguay Round agreements and at the same time combined with a strengthened liberal approach, proves that the development dimension of the Uruguay Round results is limited. The development needs and the particular problems of developing countries were addressed quite simply by writing a new set of rules on increased liberalization the way the industrialized Northern countries wanted them. And then they extended transitional periods to developing countries by way of special and differential treatment[11] because the increased liberalization was incompatible

9 *Croome, J.*, Guide to the Uruguay Round Agreements, 1999, 224.

10 *Michalopoulos, C.*, Developing Countries in the WTO, 2001, 35.

11 *Lamy, P.*, in a speech in Berlin, 28 January 2002, http://europa.eu.int/comm/commissioners/lamy/speeches_articles/spla93_en.htm (last visited 12 August 2003).

with the economic situation of the developing countries so that necessarily the liberalization had to go along with technical provisions specifically designed for developing countries.[12] Special and differential treatment was granted to the developing countries to consider their problems in implementing the obligations of the Uruguay Round agreements. This reflects the tendency not to grant developing countries broad exceptions to compliance with GATT rules[13] and has nothing to do with an attitude of considering the needs of the developing countries and then trying to find rules and norms specifically tailored to their needs. Instead the industrialized countries looked to their own needs, drafted the new rules accordingly and then conceded derogations to the weaker economies. Special and differential treatment was not integrated systematically but rather added on as an afterthought.

Nevertheless, the results of the Uruguay Round in principle were favourable to the development of the developing countries as they led to significant market access improvements in areas of interest to developing countries (agriculture, textiles, and clothing) and in an elimination of grey area measures by the Agreement on Safeguards. But the liberalization in agriculture, textiles and clothing had only a very limited degree. Furthermore, the industrialized states entered into commitments to abolish practices that violated the letter or the spirit of GATT (like the Multi-Fibre Arrangement or voluntary export restraints), but in turn received a substantial expansion of the coverage and reach of multilateral disciplines that does not take proper account of the implementation problems of developing countries.[14] This illustrates the negotiating power asymmetries.

c) The brief iteration of the evolution of world trade law clarifies that, as regards development, GATT 1947 mainly had a merely instrumental character. GATT 1947 was not designed for the purpose of developing poor states but for liberalizing world trade the side effect of which can and should be development by increasing welfare. The importance of

---

12 *Flory, M.*, New GATT and NIEO, in: *Oppermann, T./Molsberger, J.* (eds.), A new GATT for the Nineties and Europe '92, 1991, 390.

13 *Trebilcock, M./Howse, R.*, The Regulation of International Trade, 2nd edition 2000, 388.

14 *Chadha, R. et al.*, Developing Countries and the Next Round of WTO Negotiations, in: *Hoekman, B./Martin, W.* (eds.), Developing Countries and the WTO, 2001, 1 et seq; *Hertel, T./Hoekman, B./Martin, W.*, Developing Countries and a New Round of WTO Negotiations, World Bank Research Observer, 2002, 128.

GATT 1947 for development policy lay in the circumstance that it had the tools and technical machinery to implement decisions and resolutions on development issues taken at the specialized development forum that had trade relevance. GATT 1947 was merely reacting and responding to these decisions.

These deliberations in principle apply to the WTO as well. The WTO was established in order to reduce barriers to trade. This has development side-effects. But in contrast to GATT 1947, the needs of developing countries received greater attention. The negotiations about preferences for developing states took place within the Uruguay Round negotiations. Preferential treatment was not initiated from outside, but resulted from active participation of the developing states in the multilateral trade negotiations. These negotiations, however, were not driven by development concerns, but by trade and economic concerns. Additionally, the sensitivity for global coherence of economic policymaking has risen (see Article III:5 WTO Agreement). This was also endorsed in its development relevance by the Contracting Partners in the Declaration on the Contribution of the WTO to Achieving Greater Coherence in Global Economic Policymaking. The WTO as shaped at the end of the Uruguay Round was a trade organization dedicated to building a frame of barrier free trade between all of its members but had the capacity to gain a more comprehensive understanding of the development relevance of a world trading system and its development implications than ever before.

2. Doha: A new development dimension to the WTO?

The Ministerial Conferences following the Uruguay Round paid attention to the needs of the developing countries, in particular to the least developed states. The Ministerial Declaration of Singapore and the preparations for the meeting in Seattle endorsed the importance of the developing countries' fuller participation in world trade and the world trading system for their development as well as for global trade.[15] The Singapore Ministerial Conference adopted a Comprehensive and Integrated Plan of Action for the Least Developed Countries[16] in order to combat their marginalisation. These incentives referred to the developing states as WTO members that have to be integrated into the world trading system by increased market access, assisting them in implementing their WTO commitments and in capacity building. Their con-

15 WT/MIN(96)/DEC, para. 13 et seq.

16 WT/MIN(96)/14.

cern for developing states was motivated by trade objectives; again the reference to their development needs merely works as a side effect. The mandate of the WTO was not and could not be broadened. However para. 14 of the Singapore Ministerial agreed to organize a meeting with other international institutions to foster an integrated approach to assist the least developed countries in enhancing their trading opportunities the result of which became the Integrated Framework for Trade-Related Technical Assistance to Least Developed Countries.[17]

In the Doha Ministerial Conference in 2001 a new trade round, the successor to the Uruguay round, was successfully launched. The Ministerial Declaration adopted at Doha is well known as the Doha Development Agenda, which implies that the WTO got a new development dimension. There seems to be increasing consensus that the new round is a development round as it is focussing on development issues. Indeed the Agenda deals with key concerns of developing countries and gives great prominence to development concerns since it promises to place their needs at the heart of the work programme.[18] The Declaration endorses the important role of enhanced market access, balanced rules, and "well targeted, sustainably financed" technical assistance and capacity-building programmes and again gives special attention to the effective participation of the least developed states.[19] There are some more issues that are quite new and important for global development policy like debt and finances or transfer of technology (para. 36 et seq.). The Doha Agenda, however, is not only about development. It refers to other topics like services, public procurement, trade facilitation, foreign investment, competition (the four so-called Singapore issues), liberalisation of trade in goods and environment.[20] After the Singapore Ministerial Declaration established a working group on trade and investment, the Doha Ministerial Declaration provides that negotiations on investment protection will take place after the Fifth Session of the Ministerial Conference at Cancun.[21] The negotiations shall embrace the interests of both the developing and the developed states, in particular respect

---

17 See http://www.wto.org/english/tratop_e/devel_e/framework.htm and www.integrated framework.org (last visited 12 September 2003).

18 See WT/MIN(01)/DEC/1, para. 2.

19 Doha Ministerial Declaration, WT/MIN (01)/DEC/1, para. 2 et seq.

20 Doha Ministerial Declaration, 14 November 2001, WT/MIN(01)/DEC/1, para. 20-25, 31-33.

21 Doha Ministerial Declaration, 14 November 2001, WT/MIN(01)/DEC/1, para. 20.

the development policies of the host country.[22] Nevertheless – remembering the failure of the Multilateral Agreement on Investments – there is the danger that the negotiations will mainly focus on the interest of industrialized states in the protection of investments. [23]

Despite of the famous name "Doha Development Agenda" the exact meaning of the development concerns to the negotiations has yet to be defined by their outcome.[24] This is what counts. The results of the trade negotiations initiated by the Doha Agenda can bring a broadening of the WTO mandate similar to the broadening of GATT by the Uruguay Round, but the Doha Agenda still is primarily focussed on trade and trade-related subjects. The Doha Ministerial stretches out to new topics but does not constitute a development agenda. Development is not the dominant factor, but got a new impetus.[25] The Declaration stresses the importance of both the interests of developed and developing states.[26] Nevertheless, the Doha Agenda can be expected to reach more balanced negotiations and more balanced outcomes of the negotiations when compared to the Uruguay Round. It seems as if asymmetric burdens shall definitively be avoided. The post Doha negotiations could result in substantive progress from the point of view of development if the developing countries highly participate in the negotiations, if development issues remain high on the negotiating agenda and if complementing progress can be found in the additional issues that are particularly related as well to development (debt and finance, transfer of technology). The new agreements should be consistent, at least to a great extent, with development strategies and requirements.

---

22 See para. 22 of the Doha Min Declaration: "Any framework should reflect in a balanced manner the interests of home and host countries, and take due account of the development policies and objectives of host governments as well as their right to regulate in the public interest. The special development, trade and financial needs of developing and least-developed countries should be taken into account as an integral part of any framework, which should enable members to undertake obligations and commitments commensurate with their individual needs and circumstances. Due regard should be paid to other relevant WTO provisions. Account should be taken, as appropriate, of existing bilateral and regional arrangements on investment."

23 See *Subedi, S.*, The Road from Doha: The Issues for the Development Round of the WTO and the Future of International Trade, ICLQ 2003, 440.

24 *Subedi, S.*, The Road from Doha: The Issues for the Development Round of the WTO and the Future of International Trade, ICLQ 2003, 442 et seq.

25 See also *Subedi, S.*, The Road from Doha: The Issues for the Development Round of the WTO and the Future of International Trade, ICLQ 2003, 443, 446.

26 See para. 22, 49 of the Declaration.

Despite the rising importance of development issues and the increasing participation of developing states the WTO still is not a development organization. Developing less developed states is not the core business of the multilateral trading system. But the sensitivity for the importance of integrating the poor countries into the world market for their development, as well as for the sake of growth of the world economy and for world peace and security has led to greater efforts to make the WTO rules work for the developing states as well. The development dimension of the trading system seems to increase. Remarkably, the Doha Agenda calls for more coherence in international economic policymaking, which is an element of a development agenda.

III. Development Policy Objectives Covered by WTO Rules

The rules and disciplines of the WTO agreements are important for the implementation of development policies as a lot of development aims fall under the coverage of the WTO/GATT-rules. Firstly, the WTO members' implementation of obligations and commitments to liberalize and open markets promotes development aims. Even in a development perspective the fact that the WTO provides strong and enforceable rules and disciplines for international trade agreed through multilateral rather than bilateral agreement is important for developing states, even more important than for developed states, since developing states do not have enough bargaining power to influence the behaviour of others unilaterally.[27] The enforceability of the WTO rules by the dispute settlement system, which is also accessible for developing states in case of conflict with developed states, promotes rule compliance also in the interest of the poor.

Secondly, the WTO influences the development policy through the effects its rules and disciplines have upon world trade and thus upon the trade possibilities and chances of each country. The WTO leads to an increasing interdependence of economies. The increased liberalisation and opening of domestic markets produces an international interlocking influencing national economies, growth potential, employment and the margin of discretion and decision that remains to domestic economic policies. This has to be taken into account when taking development policy decisions that want to influence trade flows or the functioning and composition of domestic economies and markets or that prescribe recipes for domestic economic policies. Development prescriptions

27 *Dessus, S./Fukasaku, K./Safadi, R.*, Multilateral Tariff Liberalisation and the Developing Countries, OECD Development Centre, Policy Brief No. 18, 7 (http://www.oecd.org/document/45/0,2340,en_2649_33731_2739629_1_1_1_1,00.htm.).

and their implementation have to take care that the WTO obligations of the country they are addressed to are respected. WTO rules constrain the development policy choice in the same way as they restrict the trade policies of the WTO members themselves. That applies all the more as the Uruguay Round widened the coverage of the disciplines beyond traditional border measures into behind-the-border policies (like product standards or TRIPS) which are also linked to wider aspects of development policy.

WTO disciplines that are in line with development objectives are promoting liberalized markets and exports, reducing trade barriers and attracting capital to developing countries as a consequence of the framework of rules that increases legal certainty. Thus, not only (if at all) the special and differential treatment provisions (see IV.) do have a development dimension.

1. Developing domestic markets

The rules and disciplines of the WTO agreements help the developing states to develop their markets since the implementation of the obligations require domestic reforms that liberalize economic activities. Against the background of free trade and open markets, a domestic economic policy of self-sufficiency is no longer possible. Developing countries' industrialization and diversification improve the more they are integrated into world trade.

Low tariffs and liberalized trade ease the market access of foreign products. This can create distortions to domestic markets of the developing countries as for example low world market prices of agricultural products are transmitted to domestic markets due to the commitment to low bound tariffs. In such a situation, the developing countries would like to use border measures to safeguard against price declines in order to develop their agricultural market. The WTO agreements in general provide for means to protect domestic industries and markets in the GATT, the Agreement on Safeguards, the Agreement on Subsidies and Countervailing Measures and in the Agreement on Antidumping. There are special provisions for developing countries like GATT articles allowing for infant industry and balance of payments exceptions (Article XII, XVIII GATT, Article 4 TRIMS-Agreement).[28] Governments enjoy enough flexibility for their development politics.[29]

---

28 See *Matsushita, M./Schoenbaum, T./Mavroidis, P.*, The World Trade Organization, 2003, 380 et seq.

29 A different question is whether all of these possibilities, especially the contingent protection, are beneficial to world trade and the developing countries in particular.

2. *Raising exports*

WTO rules provide for easier access to foreign markets, in particular to those of the developed states. The Uruguay Round agreements reduced tariffs and non-tariff barriers to trade. As a consequence of the Uruguay Round agreements the degree of tariff escalation[30] has decreased, but it is still a matter of concern in certain products in respect of market access for developing-country exports.[31] It makes market access more difficult for finished manufactured products, which in turn adversely affects developing countries' industrialization efforts.

Market access of products that are of particular export interest to the developing countries (textiles, clothing, and agricultural products) has been increased but still can be improved. From 1 January 2005 on, for example, textiles and clothing will be integrated into GATT and will therefore no longer be subject to special rules to the detriment of the developing countries.[32]

Regarding the ban of export subsidies, developing countries enjoy some privileges.[33] The ban on export subsidies does not apply to least developed countries. Furthermore, export subsidies are still allowed in the Agreement on Agriculture. Regional economic integration is acceptable due to Article XXIV GATT so that developing states can increase their exports by building free trade areas or customs unions.[34] Again there are preferential rules as regards developing countries. WTO rules enable tariff and non-tariff preferences to developing countries and special schemes for the least developed countries (Enabling Clause).

---

30 Tariff escalation increases the rate of effective protection at higher stages of processing as the customs for them are comparatively higher than customs for primary commodities.

31 *Michalopoulos, C.*, Developing Countries in the WTO, 2001, 108.

32 *Weiß, W./Herrmann, C.*, Welthandelsrecht, 2003, Mn. 113, 725 et seq.

33 See Article 27 Agreement on Subsidies and Countervailing Measures; *Matsushita, M./Schoenbaum, T./Mavroidis, P.*, The World Trade Organization, 2003, 266, 387; *Weiß, W./Herrmann, C.*, Welthandelsrecht, 2003, Mn. 703.

34 For more detail on the developmental benefits as well as risks of regional integration see *Hoekman, B.*, Strengthening the Global Trade Architecture for Development: the Post Doha Agenda, WTR 2002, 39 et seq.

IV. Preferential, Special and Differential Treatment of Developing States

One result of UNCTAD was to embed in the GATT the broad concept of non-reciprocity and "special and differential treatment" for developing countries.[35] Special and differential treatment and other WTO rules granting exceptions to the developing states were founded on a development paradigm that stressed the need for domestic industrial policy and protection for import-competing industries as well as the need to deal with balance of payments volatility[36] and as a consequence of the WTO disciplines on behind-the-border measures gained a new quality and importance. In the area of special and differential treatment, the development dimension of the WTO can be linked to the issue of the right to development which is best understood as a "right to a particular process of development" which by corollary requires the elimination of obstacles to development.[37] Apart from proposing a wide-ranging programmatic approach to development, the right to development does not specify in much operational detail what these obstacles are. Trade barriers for sure are such obstacles. Thus, the WTO objective of liberalizing trade conforms to the right to development.[38] Since the special and differential treatment provisions in WTO agreements are already more specific than the right to development, this right cannot help to add more contractual detail to the existing special and differential treatment provisions.[39] Special and differential treatment of developing country members, however, implicates a certain tension regarding the objective of full integration of developing countries to the international trading system, since members that are treated differently to others might not fully participate. Preferential treatment that results in avoidance of liberalisation commitments and market opening obligations can even retard development.

Currently, there are 155 individual references to special and differential treatment of the developing countries in the WTO agreements.[40] Those preferences granted to the developing states work in different ways[41]:

---

35 For an analysis of the evolution of non-reciprocity and preferential treatment see *Hudec, R.*, Developing Countries in the GATT Legal System, 1987

36 *Ostry, S.*, The Uruguay Round North-South Grand Bargain: Implications for Future Negotiations, 2000, 12.

37 See *Sengupta, A.*, Study on the Current State of Progress in the Implementation of the Right to Development, UN Document E/CN.4/1999/WG.18/2, 4, 10.

38 *Lim, H.*, Trade and Human Rights: What's at Issue?, JWT 2001, 293.

39 *Lim, H.*, Trade and Human Rights: What's at Issue?, JWT 2001, 297.

40 *WTO, Committee on Trade and Development*, Implementation of Special and Differential Treatment Provisions in WTO Agreements and Decisions, WT/COMTD/

1. Developed countries providing preferential treatment

Developed countries provide developing states with three types of special treatment:

a) *Firstly*, trade opportunities of developing country members are increased. They get non-reciprocal preferential market access by the Generalized System of Preferences (GSP) if the developed member states are willing to grant preferential treatment (they are not required to do so). The GSP allows for tariff and non-tariff preferences and an even increased special treatment of least developed states. In practice, the developed states granted tariff, but not non-tariff preferences. The preferences result in increased market access to industrialized states' markets and in a diversification of developing countries' exports into manufactured products.

b) *Secondly,* the developing states receive more favourable treatment in the implementation of Uruguay Round agreements. These agreements contain many references both in preambles and in substantive provisions allowing or obliging developed members to implement the agreements in ways that safeguard the interests of the developing states and the least developed ones among them. Some of these references are general in nature and are "best efforts" obligations of sole exhortatory nature[42], but a few are clearer[43]. Thus, the particular interests of the developing states were recognized by the developed states.

c) *Thirdly*, the developing states get technical assistance by the developed states to help them implement their Uruguay round commitments.[44] Such assistance aims at strengthening the institutional capacity in order to enable them to meet the obligations they have assumed under the WTO agreements since it is easy to formulate policies to liberalize trade, but it is far more difficult to develop the capacity to take advantage of the opportunities international trade provides. Institutional constraints significantly inhibit the effective integration of developing countries in the trading system. Technical assistance (as well as longer transition periods) addresses the weaknesses in the infrastructure and institutions related to international trade that have been identified as key impediments in developing coun-

---

W/77/Rev.1, 14. There one can find a detailed analysis of the agreements in this regard.

41 See also the typology of special and differential treatment provisions given in *WTO*, World Trade Report 2003, 155 et seq.

42 See e.g. Art. 12.2 TBT

43 *Michalopoulos, C.*, Developing Countries in the WTO, 2001, 37 et seq.

44 *Michalopoulos, C.*, Developing Countries in the WTO, 2001, 36 et seq; 200.

tries' capacities to benefit from international trade.[45] Usually, assistance is provided upon request by the developing country and on terms and conditions mutually agreed upon.[46]

2. *Differential commitments and obligations of developing states*

a) The obligations of developing states resulting from their commitment to the WTO agreements are different to those of developed states. There are two fundamental ways to lower their commitments:[47]

aa) *First:* Their obligations and commitments are either different or less restrictive compared to those of the industrialized member states (flexibility of commitments). They may undertake policies that limit access to their markets or allow for support of domestic producers or exporters in a way not allowed to other members (exemption from disciplines; protection of domestic industry).

One has to see, however, that in economic theory, exemptions of obligations that intend to encourage countries' progress toward better economic policy (e.g. restraints of export subsidies), are harmful.[48] They hinder sound economic policy in the developing states and thus are counterproductive because domestic groups will urge to make usage of the possibilities. Special and differential treatment provisions do not always make sense.

bb) *Second*: The Uruguay Round agreements grant special implementation periods to developing states so that they have more time to meet their obligations.

b) Pursuant to the mandate provided by some Uruguay Round agreements and decisions such as the Decision on Measures in Favour of Least Developed Countries, a variety of technical assistance activities and programs are provided to developing countries by the WTO[49] and even international organizations outside the WTO (UNCTAD, ITC and the

---

45 *Michalopoulos, C.*, The Role of Special and Differential Treatment for Developing Countries in GATT and the World Trade Organization, World Bank Policy Research Working Paper No. 2388, 2000, 16 et seq.

46 E.g. Article 9.1 SPS; Article 11, 12.7 TBT; Article 20.3 Agreement on the Implementation of GATT Article VII (Customs Valuation); Article 3.3 Agreement on Pre-Shipment Inspection; Article 67 TRIPS.

47 *Michalopoulos, C.*, Developing Countries in the WTO, 2001, 38.

48 *Finger, M./Winters, A.*, What Can the WTO do for Developing Countries?, in: *Krueger, A.* (ed.), The WTO as International Organization, 1998, 386.

49 See e.g. Art. 27.2 DSU.

World Bank). As already mentioned, the latter two elements (transitional periods, technical assistance) were introduced by the Uruguay Round.

3. Special measures for least developed countries

The least developed states, i.e. those developing states that are extremely poor, have a special status as they receive even more preferences (e. g. longer transitional period; special attention to their needs). Within the groups of special and differential treatment provisions indicated above there are additional provisions which relate specifically to the least developed countries.[50]

V. Continuing Challenges to WTO's Development Dimension

Free trade is a continuing challenge as the WTO rules at their current state do not liberalize all trade and as the commitments for improved market access have to be implemented. The Uruguay Round rules have to be improved for the sake of legal certainty and clarity and in order to better serve their purpose. The nature of WTO rules, the reach of these rules, and the conditions of market access are the three major areas that determine the quality and utility of the WTO for its members. Not surprisingly, each of these three elements features prominently in the Doha Development Agenda.[51] For example, the use of contingent protection enabled through safeguard or antidumping measures has to be disciplined as it reduces the value of trade liberalisation. This topic is on the Doha Agenda.[52] These challenges are general to the WTO and basically concern the developing states in the same way as developed states. Development needs however place some particular challenges to the treatment of developing states by WTO law.

The following proposals try to suggest some improvements of the world trade system that enable the WTO to contribute more effectively to development.

1. Heterogeneity of developing states

Developing countries are very heterogeneous and are not in the same situation. Their capacity to export and compete in international markets differs vastly. Therefore, the degree of assistance they need to break into foreign markets is

---

50 See e.g. Articles 21.8, 24.1 and 24.2 DSU. For more details see *Michalopoulos, C.*, Developing Countries in the WTO, 2001, 41 et seq.

51 *WTO*, World Trade Report 2003, 118.

52 See WT(MIN(01)/DEC/1, para. 28.

very different.[53] The WTO rules on developing countries do not reflect these differences (apart from special rules for least developed countries; in the Agreement on Subsidies and Countervailing Measures, a special differentiation on per capita income has been established). The Enabling Clause incorporated the issue of *graduation* and the WTO law requires the developing states to contribute to trade liberalization according to their level of development. The problem, however, is that there are no clear-cut WTO rules on this issue. The developing countries have been treated differently by industrialized states in their unilateral implementation of GSP.[54]

2. *Reshaping special and differential treatment*

Special and differential treatment provisions need reshaping for different reasons while flexibility has to be maintained. The Doha Agenda particularly focuses on special and differential treatment provisions and calls for a review in order to strengthen them and to make them more precise, effective and operational.[55]

First of all, as already indicated special and differential treatment provisions do not reflect the heterogeneity of developing states. One size does not fit all.[56] Secondly, already mentioned as well, some preferential rules are *counterproductive* as they might strengthen domestic protectionist interest groups. Not all preferences work for the good of the developing states and their development. The idea that less engagement in the WTO means more development is a fallacy.[57] It has to be considered whether special and differential treatment is in the interest of developing countries as it hinders their full integration into the multilateral trading system. To lag behind in the implementation of WTO Agreements might delay economic reforms and is negative for the future evolution of the multilateral trading system. Delay makes compliance increasingly difficult and may deny the developing states the chance to influence the direction of future negotiations. Therefore, the disadvantageous provisions (e.g. those providing greater flexibility to protect domestic markets or

---

53 *Michalopoulos, C.*, Developing Countries in the WTO, 2001, 201.

54 *Michalopoulos, C.*, Developing Countries in the WTO, 2001, 202.

55 See Doha Ministerial Declaration, para. 44; *Hart, M./Dymond, B.*, Special and Differential Treatment and the Doha "Development" Round, JWT 2003, 395.

56 See *Stevens, C.*, If One Size Doesn't Fit All, What Does? Rethinking Special and Differential Treatment in the WTO, IDS Bulletin Vol. 34, No. 2, 2003.

57 *Hart, M./Dymond, B.*, Special and Differential Treatment and the Doha "Development" Round, JWT 2003, 395; *Hudec, R.*, Developing Countries in the GATT legal system, 1987, 151, 227; *WTO*, World Trade Report 2003, 151 et seq.

subsidise exports) have to be identified and to be removed or altered. Transition periods might also be inadequate, as they seem to be somewhat arbitrary; at least they can be improved by provisions that provide for an extension of the periods on case by case basis (see e.g. Article 20 Agreement on Implementation of Article VII GATT (Customs Valuation); Article 5.3 TRIM's Agreement [Trade Related Investment Measures' Agreement]). Special and differential treatment, however, is particularly important in areas where the WTO rules lead to positive prescriptions that enforce domestic regulatory reforms (e.g. TRIPS [Trade-related Intellectual Property Rights]) because they challenge the implementation endeavours of the developing countries much more because the human resources to administer such regimes might not be available.[58] WTO disciplines of this type might not work for development to the same extent as rules on traditional border measures.[59] Thus, preferential treatment of the developing states in these areas is much more necessary, particularly as regards the implementation of rules on behind-the-border measures.

Regarding the implementation of commitments of the developed states in favour of developing states we could see that *"Best efforts" commitments* were made in practically all WTO agreements. The problem of these provisions is that they do not lead to specific obligations to take or not to take a certain measure.[60] Due to this lack of clarity, developed states failed to implement them;[61] at least their observance can hardly be examined.

Another problematic field are the *GSP preferences*. The economic benefits of the GSP are of limited value for most developing states and the preferences are not fully applied in a generalized, non-discriminatory and non-reciprocal way, being the main GSP principles according to UNCTAD Resolution of 1968.[62] The benefits of the GSP have eroded because of the MFN tariff reduction (preference margins have reduced as a consequence of the Uruguay

---

58 *Hart, M./Dymond, B.*, Special and Differential Treatment and the Doha "Development" Round, JWT 2003, 398, 408 et seq.

59 *Hoekman, B.*, Strengthening the Global Trade Architecture for Development: the Post Doha Agenda, WTR 2002, 27 et seq., 31 et seq.

60 See regarding Article 15 of the Antidumping Code *Weiß, W./Herrmann, C.*, Welthandelsrecht, 2003, Mn. 678.

61 *Michalopoulos, C.*, Developing Countries in the WTO, 2001, 198

62 UNCTAD Resolution 21 (II). Regarding these principles see *Petersmann, E.-U.*, International Economic Law and International Economic Order, in: *Oppermann, T./Petersmann, E.-U.* (eds.), Reforming the International Economic Order, 1987, 225.

Round tariff reduction[63]) and the increasing limitations contained in the schemes: They are unbound, thus reversible; many are subject to quantitative limits; they contain limitations regarding products (products often excluded are those of special interest for the developing countries; another contentious issue is the applicable rule of origin) and country eligibility by the graduation features of various preferential programmes.[64] As the Enabling Clause does not indicate criteria for graduation, the preferential schemes can do so. Finally, the GSP may result in wrong types of dependencies in terms of concentration of economic activity in preference-receiving industries, a lack of dynamism and vulnerability and may retard rather than promote their integration into the international trading system.[65] Thus it is doubtful whether GSP remains a valuable tool to promote developing countries' exports.[66] At least, the serious flaws and limitations in the existing trade preference systems should be addressed before embarking on new preferential trade initiatives for poor countries.[67] Moreover, additional regional preferential arrangements that provide deeper and more secure preferences have been put in place so that the prefer-

---

63 *Michalopoulos, C.*, Developing Countries in the WTO, 2001, 201. *Finger, M./ Winters, A.*, What Can the WTO do for Developing Countries?, in: *Krueger, A.* (ed.), The WTO as International Organization, 1998, 384, however, state that the erosion of GSP preference margins were not very significant, apart from few exceptions.

64 *Finger, M./Winters, A.*, What Can the WTO do for Developing Countries?, in *Krueger, A.* (ed.), The WTO as International Organization, 1998, 385; *Michalopoulos, C.*, Developing Countries in the WTO, 2001, 106.

65 *Michalopoulos, C.*, Developing Countries in the WTO, 2001, 106.

66 As say UNCTAD/WTO, Market Access Developments since the Uruguay Round: Implications, Opportunities and Challenges, in Particular for Developing Countries and Least Developed Countries, in the Context of Globalization and Liberalization, 1997, p. 9.

67 A recent analysis into the effect of agreements which allow imports of developing countries' products to enter developed countries at a lower tariff rate finds that generally trade preferences schemes are not that beneficial to very poor countries. In cases where the benefits are significant, there are also significant costs. Moreover, they may provide benefits to only one group of poor countries at the expense of others. The report also warns that trade preferences may be used to obtain external support for protectionist policies, which can be used to impede global trade liberalisation efforts. See the report "Trade Preferences: Are They Helpful in Advancing Economic Development in Poor Countries?" by the Australian Bureau of Agriculture and Resource Economics as of November 2001, available on www.abareconomics.com. The report focuses on the US, EU, Japan and Canada, but notes that there are a large number of trade preference systems in operation which vary by countries covered, products covered, the size of the tariff preferences on offer and many other conditions. See also http://www.worldgrowth.org/pages/trade/wg-doha.shtml.

ences of the GSP have become less important.[68] Moreover, the developing states have to be aware that due to the considerable reduction of tariffs and non-tariff barriers they have to compete on the basis of economic factors rather than special treatment.[69]

The right to development cannot help to further strengthen the special and differential treatment provisions due to the considerable lack of clarity on what the right to development means as a legal concept or on how it can be operationalized. Without greater clarification on this, the right to development cannot contribute to the reshaping of special and differential treatment.

3. *Assisting developing countries in their endeavours*

The endeavours of the developing countries to become *integrated into world trade* must be assisted in a better way. Assistance should focus on export promotion (by taking care of supply side constraints such as bad quality of products, low productivity and diversification that impede making use of preferential market access; this however is not covered by the ambit of the WTO) and increased access to developed countries' markets for products and manufactured goods of particular export interest to developing states. That calls for progressive trade liberalisation and market opening by developed states (reduction of tariff peaks and tariff escalation)[70] including generous market opening for least developed countries.[71] The Doha Agenda promises limited progress insofar.[72] Recent research suggests that there is still a large market

68 *Michalopoulos, C.*, Developing Countries in the WTO, 2001, 201. The Enabling Clause also relaxed the conditions for creating free trade areas or customs unions (Art.. XXIV GATT) that include only developing countries. South-south arrangements are, however, only of limited economic interest.

69 See *Onguglo, B. F.*, Developing Countries and Trade Preferences, in: *Mendoza, M. et al.* (eds.), Trade Rules in the Making, 1999, 132.

70 These are still a problem to developing countries' exports, see *Onguglo, B. F.*, Developing Countries and Trade Preferences, in: *Mendoza, M. et al.* (eds.), Trade Rules in the Making, 1999, 121 et seq.

71 *Wiemann, J.*, Developing Countries and WTO Round: Winners or losers? Or: Winners and losers?, paper presented at a conference organized by the research institute of the Deutsche Gesellschaft für Auswärtige Politik, available on http://www.dgap.org (last visited 22 August 2003).

72 See para. 16 regarding market access of non-agricultural products: The negotiations shall aim "to reduce or as appropriate eliminate tariffs, including the reduction or elimination of tariff peaks, high tariffs, and tariff escalation, as well as non-tariff barriers, in particular on products of export interest to developing countries. Product coverage shall be comprehensive and without a priori exclusions."

access agenda and that the potential gains in particular for developing countries from further liberalization of trade both in agriculture and industrial products (three quarters of their exports are manufactures) remain very large.[73] In addition, present rules have to be examined under the point of view of which adjustments are necessary to respond to the needs of developing countries. Priority should be given to ensuring that rules are consistent with the development needs of poorer countries and to helping developing countries implement WTO obligations.[74] The content of future WTO obligations should not be tailored according to the concepts of advanced nations as it happened in Uruguay Round.[75] This is a peculiar danger if disciplines on behind-the-border measures are introduced.[76]

The needs of the least developed countries deserve special attention. The Doha Agenda recognizes that their "integration into the multilateral trading system requires meaningful market access, support for the diversification of their production and export base, and trade-related technical assistance and capacity building." The agenda aims at duty-free, quota-free market access for products originating from least developed states.[77] Against the background of existing tariff peaks and tariff escalation that have a disproportionate negative impact particularly on the exports of the least developed states[78] this is an ambitious objective.

The diversification of developing countries' economies is promoted by new dimensions to the *free trade in services*: Many developing countries are now aware that trade in services can provide significant export opportunities if there is more liberalization for labour access which refers to the fourth mode of supplying services, i.e. the temporary posting of service workers (see Article I:2 d GATS). This can be viewed as rebalancing since the (understandable) priority of industrialized countries has been access for foreign direct in-

---

73 *Hertel, T./Hoekman, B./Martin, W.*, Developing Countries and a New Round of WTO Negotiations, World Bank Research Observer, 2002, 121 et seq., 134.

74 *Hertel, T./Hoekman, B./Martin, W.*, Developing Countries and a New Round of WTO Negotiations, World Bank Research Observer, 2002, 129.

75 *Finger, M./Schuler, P.*, Implementation of Uruguay Round Commitments: The Development Challenge, in: *Hoekman, B./Martin, W.* (eds.), Developing Countries and the WTO, 2001, 126; *Hertel, T./Hoekman, B./Martin, W.*, Developing Countries and a New Round of WTO Negotiations, World Bank Research Observer, 2002, 129.

76 See also *Hoekman, B.*, Strengthening the Global Trade Architecture for Development, WTR 2002, 27.

77 Doha Ministerial Declaration, para. 42.

78 *Hertel, T./Hoekman, B./Martin, W.*, Developing Countries and a New Round of WTO Negotiations, World Bank Research Observer, 2002, 134.

vestment (Article I:2 c GATS).[79] A number of developing countries have a comparative advantage in the labour component of service production in sectors such as construction, transport, distribution and software. An increased liberalisation of services may, however, be difficult because of the extreme sensitivity of the immigration issue in Europe, which will generate pressure to include some form of labour standards for temporary movements.[80] Very little, if anything, was done in the Uruguay Round to enhance developing country service export opportunities.[81] Services liberalization nevertheless is vital to economic growth in developing countries.[82] In order to meet the concerns of the developed countries, one could tie a safeguard instrument to mode liberalization commitments.[83] Para. 15 of the Doha Declaration states that negotiations on services shall promote the growth of all and the development of developing countries.

Another proposal to promote developing countries' endeavours would be to attribute a *policy advice role* to the WTO in order to improve market liberalisation.[84] Adapting the WTO Trade Policy Reviews to the needs of developing countries could support this.[85] On the other hand the World Bank might be the

79 See *Hertel, T./Hoekman, B./Martin, W.*, Developing Countries and a New Round of WTO Negotiations, World Bank Research Observer, 2002, 124.

80 *Ostry, S.*, The Uruguay Round North-South Grand Bargain: Implications for Future Negotiations, 2000, 20 et seq.; *Weiß, W./Herrmann, C.*, Welthandelsrecht 2003, Mn. 845, 872 et seq.

81 *Chadha, R. et al.*, Developing Countries and the Next Round of WTO Negotiations, in: *Hoekman, B./Martin, W.* (eds.), Developing Countries and the WTO, 2001, 3.

82 *Mbekeani, K. K.*, GATS Negotiations Must Focus on Services Liberalization: The Case of SADC, in: July 2003 issue of the World Bank publication Development Outreach, available on http://www.worldbank.org/devoutreach/article.asp?id=208 (last visited 12 September 2003), outlines the importance of current GATS negotiations in the WTO. *Mbekeani* explains how reforms in sectors such as financial services, telecommunications and transport facilitate growth and economic efficiency. In particular, the availability of infrastructure and financial services attracts investment and supports export industries. The challenge for developing countries is to negotiate services liberalization that leads to the transfer of technology and capacity-building.

83 *Hertel, T./Hoekman, B./Martin, W.*, Developing Countries and a New Round of WTO Negotiations, World Bank Research Observer, 2002, 126.

84 See *Alan Hirsch*, Comment on the Paper by Michael Finger and Alan Winters, in: *Krueger, A.* (ed.), The WTO as an International Organization, 1998, 395. The Trade Policy Reports do not assess the compatibility of the described policies with WTO obligations.

85 See *Borrmann, A./Koopmann, G.*, Adapting the WTO Trade Policy Reviews to the Needs of Developing Countries, 2002.

institution better equipped for that, especially since one should avoid doubling competences.

In helping the developing countries to strengthen their capacity to *participate* more effectively in the trading system, the *working methods* of the WTO and the challenge of ensuring that all parties to the WTO agreements are given an adequate opportunity to participate in deliberations, make their voices heard and influence outcomes are as well important.[86] The Doha Ministerial Declaration, however, did not put the issue of improving the working methods of the WTO on the agenda.[87] Considering the broader and broader WTO agenda one must state that the traditional GATT way of decision-making does not correspond to it given that behind-the-border measures require more intensive involvement of the developing countries as they place a higher burden on their implementation efforts.

The participation of the developing states will also benefit from a clear understanding of their own national development objectives and priorities. This requires increased assistance and research support for the developing countries in order to enable them to define national objectives and to make them understand how the WTO disciplines help them in their attainment. Furthermore, it calls for greater involvement of domestic constituents that have interests in cross border trade.[88] The latter will also lead to extended support for the necessary domestic reforms and the implementation efforts of developing countries.

4. *Improving technical assistance*

Developing countries need capacities to analyse issues and mechanisms to feed this analysis into their implementation efforts and into a process of decision-making that in turn is fed to the negotiators. Otherwise they can only pursue a delay strategy (by transition periods). In the Uruguay Round a pro-active constructive approach was frequently out of reach for many developing countries due to their lack of research capacities and resources.[89] An important step in this direction was the establishment of the inter-governmental Agency

---

86 As for proposals for greater participation of developing countries in the WTO see *Hoekman, B.*, Strengthening the Global Trade Architecture for Development: the Post Doha Agenda, WTR 2002, 30 et seq.

87 *WTO*, World Trade Report 2003, 154.

88 *Hoekman, B.*, Strengthening the Global Trade Architecture for Development: the Post Doha Agenda, WTR 2002, 30.

89 *Chadha, R. et al.*, Developing Countries and the Next Round of WTO Negotiations, in: *Hoekman, B./Martin, W.* (eds.), Developing Countries and the WTO, 2001, 2.

for International Trade Information and Cooperation (AITIC) at Doha that provides training and assistance for delegations of developing countries to the WTO.

As 29 of the WTO members are least developed countries and two thirds of the whole membership are developing countries technical assistance offered to the developing states still is insufficient and must be remarkably improved.[90] It has to be made legally binding. The Doha Declaration calls for additional technical assistance in most areas dealt with. It urges the development partners to significantly increase contributions to the Integrated Framework and WTO extra-budgetary trust funds in favour of least developed countries. The states showed awareness of the need for considerable improvement.[91]

5. *Implementation of developing countries' obligations*

The developing countries must be assisted in implementing the obligations entered into by them. Because of the above explained techniques how the special and differential treatment provisions were introduced in the WTO agreements, it is not at all surprising that the developing countries still do have difficulties in implementing the Uruguay Round Agreements. The Uruguay Round requirements do not identify the problems that exist in developing countries and they consequently demand the institutions and regulations that will impose higher costs than benefits on the countries that implement them.[92] The implementation issue soon became a major element in the discussions after the Uruguay Round. This issue is closely related to the demand for considerably *improved technical assistance*. There is a need for funds for developing states to enable them to effectuate the full implementation; development assistance should be given by the developed states for that purpose. The Doha Ministerial Declaration (para. 12) endorsed the decision on "Implementation-Related Issues and Concerns"[93] that settled some problems by adopting about fifty decisions clarifying the obligations of developing country members and introduced negotiations regarding the remaining more vital concerns. It made negotiations on outstanding implementation issues an integral part of the Work Programme of the new trade negotiations.

---

90 *Michalopoulos, C.*, Developing Countries in the WTO, 2001, 198.

91 See para. 2, 41-43 of the Ministerial Declaration.

92 *Finger, M.*, Implementing the Uruguay Round Agreements: Problems for Developing Countries, The World Economy, vol. 24, 2001, 1097.

93 WT/MIN(01)/17.

Other aspects of implementation relate to the WTO rules themselves. There might be a need – as developing countries say – for modifications to many provisions in order to make them more operationally effective to support development or less restrictive in relation to the degree of policy flexibility.[94]

6. Increased coherence in international economic policies

The WTO was founded to cooperate with IMF and World Bank with a view to achieving greater coherence in global economic policymaking (see Article III WTO-Agreement). The aim of greater coherence in global economic policymaking was endorsed by the respective declaration at the end of the Uruguay Round.[95] Coherence in international economic policy making has also been strongly emphasized by the Doha Declaration in general terms (para. 5), regarding debt and finances (para. 36) and technical assistance and capacity building (para. 39) where a particularly intensive cooperation already exists in form of the Integrated Framework that embeds trade strategy into a development framework and coordinates support. Taking into account the development issue and introducing a closer relationship with UNCTAD could enlarge the coherence in international economics. Another way of increasing coherence within the WTO mandate could be realized within the WTO administration and the technical assistance organized by the WTO. The administration of the WTO agreements should not be carried out in a fragmented way.[96] The issue-by-issue approach of technical assistance – reflected in the Doha Declaration[97] – has to be replaced by linkage.

Since the WTO is open for coherence, it has the capacity to cooperate in a comprehensive development agenda that addresses the development of developing countries from different aspects, not only from the perspective of liberalized cross-border trade. Since such an overall development agenda is not covered by the mandate and the competences of the WTO it can only be attained by a concerted action of the relevant international institutions and organizations bringing together their competences and expertise with the WTO

94 *WTO*, World Trade Report 2003, 154.

95 Declaration on the Contribution of the WTO to Achieving Greater Coherence in Global Economic Policymaking.

96 *Breckenridge, A.*, Developing an Issues-Based Approach to Special and Differential Treatment, Working Paper for the Inter-American Development Bank, 13, available on http://www.iadb.org/int/DRP/ing/Red1/documents/Breckenbridge%20Ing.pdf (last visited 23 August 2003).

97 *Hoekman, B.*, Strengthening the Global Trade Architecture for Development: the Post Doha Agenda, WTR 2002, 42.

being the organization competent for international trade and trade-related issues. Any development agenda of the WTO can only address trade issues. Accordingly, the Doha Declaration stressed that recommendations on steps to be taken as regards the interrelationship between trade, debt and finance or trade and technology transfer have to be taken within the mandate of the WTO (see para. 36 et seq.). The WTO is prepared to contribute to coherence of international policies in these areas but will not exceed its competences. The same applies for the work programme regarding least developed countries that has to take into account the trade-related elements of the Brussels Declaration and Programme of Action, adopted at the Third UN Conference on least developed countries. Here again conformity of all action with the WTO's mandate is observed diligently (see para. 42).

Thus, the most important contribution of the WTO to development remains to improve market access conditions for goods and services and to ensure that trade rules are useful to developing countries. A full development agenda could only be implemented by the WTO if its mandate covered all development issues. That is not desirable. Of course, the evolution of world trade law has already witnessed new issues taken up by the GATT/WTO. But as its expertise is in the field of trade, it should be limited to trade and such issues directly or closely related to trade. From a development perspective, it is not advisable for the WTO to stretch the trade negotiating agenda too far. The benefits in coherence by cross-issue linkage and the increased potential gains from trade if the WTO embraces more regulatory issues that harmonizes behind-the-border measures (like labour, social or environment standards) would be outweighed by the costs: Negotiations of disciplines on domestic regulation divert attention from issues of greater development relevance. The implementation costs of such disciplines for developing countries are higher because they often lack experience and because the adopted rules tend to reflect the status quo of the developed states. Therefore, the disciplines are alien to the developing states resulting in a lack of ownership. Finally, such standards might not work for the development of the developing states as they have different development needs. The payoffs of disciplines on domestic regulatory regimes are much less certain.[98] Therefore, the cooperation on and harmonization of regulatory regimes that are not closely related to trade and where it is

98 See for more detail *Hoekman, B.*, Strengthening the Global Trade Architecture for Development: the Post Doha Agenda, WTR 2002, 27 et seq., 31 et seq.; *Hertel, T./Hoekman, B./Martin, W.*, Developing Countries and a New Round of WTO Negotiations, World Bank Research Observer, 2002, 121.

not clear that all WTO members (including developing states) will gain, is better done outside the WTO.[99]

7. *Supportive role of UNCTAD*

The issue of strengthening international coherence leads to the issue of the future role of the UNCTAD and its relationship to the WTO. The UNCTAD may be useful in order to provide technical assistance to developing countries in their participation in WTO negotiations as regards development needs. UNCTAD was already given a supportive role for the developing states in the Uruguay Round as the Secretary-General of UNCTAD had to provide technical assistance to them in order to facilitate their effective participation.[100]
The WTO could undertake a broad program of capacity building in cooperation with UNCTAD.[101] In this regard the UNCTAD could work as a forum for analyses, research and consent finding on development issues working mainly in the interest of developing countries in order to enable the south to participate in world trade in a better way and to find and articulate their positions in trade negotiations within WTO, as an "OECD of the south"[102]. In this understanding, the UNCTAD would not form a counterpart to the WTO and was not called to develop alternatives to the WTO but to support the developing countries in their efforts in WTO trade negotiations. The UNCTAD could be very helpful to further develop concepts already stemming from UNCTAD and taken over into GATT (like the Enabling Cause or the global system of trade preferences between developing states). It could assist in formulating proposals for preferential rules of origin, operationalizing best effort provisions on special and differential treatment or protecting traditional knowledge. The WTO has already referred to the work of UNCTAD on several occasions. Regarding the relationship between trade and investment, the WTO Singapore Ministerial Declaration in 1997 established a working group that was supposed to consider the respective work done in UNCTAD. The WTO Ministerial Declaration of Doha intended for negotiations in this area in September 2003 after the Fifth Ministerial Conference in Cancun and added that technical

---

99 *Hoekman, B.*, Strengthening the Global Trade Architecture for Development, World Bank Policy Research Working Paper No 2757, 12.

100 See Final Act of UNCTAD VII (1987), No. 105 (9).

101 *Ostry, S.*, The Uruguay Round North-South Grand Bargain: Implications for Future Negotiations, 2000, 17.

102 See also *Falk, R.*, Handelspolitik an der UNO vorbei? Deutscher "Weltmarktfundamentalismus" und Vereinte Nationen, in: UN-williges Deutschland. Der WEED-Report zur deutschen UNO-Politik, 1997, 80.

assistance and capacity building in this area shall be done in cooperation with other relevant intergovernmental organisations, including UNCTAD, and through appropriate regional and bilateral channels, to provide strengthened and adequately resourced assistance to respond to the needs of developing countries.[103]

VI. Final Remarks

The WTO is not a forum to formulate development strategies and aims, but it has a development relevance because it implements trade related development objectives like increased market access for developing countries' goods and services or the reform of domestic economic policy. Since the sensitivity for the developing countries has increased, the development dimension of the international trading system is rising. Nevertheless, the WTO in its current shape mainly is a factor for development policy, not an actor of it. In order for a development round (in the true sense) to become meaningful, one has to address a lot of issues that are totally divert (like e.g. exchange rate, education, population or human rights) and/or fall completely outside the ambit of the WTO although they are important for development.[104] Greater coherence between WTO international trade disciplines and other international and domestic policies relevant for development would be necessary because the needs of developing countries can only be met by a comprehensive and integrative approach that cares about the peculiar development needs and has an overview on development objectives and international obligations. This approach has to be done on a country-by-country basis. Such overall approach allows considering the problems of implementing the WTO obligations, the development priorities and the available resources at the same time. Trade policy reforms then can – as they have to – be embedded in a wider policy framework with the overall aim of development. This ensures the complement of different actions. The consequence of such approaches would be that developing countries can and have to concentrate on core areas of reform. This has to be reflected in their duty to implement WTO obligations: A developing country has to im-

103 WT/MIN(01)/DEC/1, para. 21 et seq.

104 See e.g. regarding human rights the Declaration of the 1995 Copenhagen Summit on Social Development (A/CONF.166/9, http://www.un.org/esa/socdev/wssd/agreements/decpartc.htm). According to Principle 9 of Part C human rights are important for economic development. That implies that freedom of trade should be interpreted and applied in the context of a social and international order with respect for human rights, *De Waart, P.*, Quality of Life at the Mercy of WTO panels, in: *Weiss, F./Denters/De Waart, P.* (eds.), International Economic Law with a Human Face, 1998, 109.

plement only those disciplines that correspond to its development objectives. Countries can implement their obligations at different speeds. Such concept of flexibility would really be in the interest of developing states.

Thus, a really development-oriented trade policy would lead to a much broader and more complex agenda than Doha because enhancing the trade and export capacities of a developing country involves a complex set of issues. Many aspects of a development agenda would have to be addressed outside the WTO, since a comprehensive approach would focus on different aspects like institutional reforms in the developing states in order to increase capacities, governance, domestic economic policy making with participation of stakeholders in international trade, monetary and fiscal reforms, regulatory reforms, improving infrastructure, combating corruption, improving investment climate; distortion free tax regimes. Trade reform is only one part of the task.[105] Furthermore, the approach would have to include development finance and technology policies. In order to deal with such a broad agenda for each country individually, different institutions and development donors have to be actively involved and have to cooperate. In addition to the WTO efforts to increase its development dimension as proposed above (V.), a concerted action of the international community institutions outside the WTO including unilateral actions by both industrial and developing countries is required in order to complement the results of WTO trade negotiations to make the Doha round a real development round. From a development perspective this would be the best case; it is, however, not the responsibility of the WTO. The developing states would gain much even if only the WTO improved its development dimension in the current round of multilateral negotiations according to a sincere understanding of the tasks posed by the Doha Ministerial Declaration. Currently, this seems to be closer in reach and more realistic than to advocate a case for a best development approach.

---

105 See *Hart, M./Dymond, B.*, Special and Differential Treatment and the Doha "Development" Round, JWT 2003, 408 et seq.

DISCUSSION

Professor Dr. Bernd *von Hoffmann* (Trier) started the discussion, alluding to the roles of agriculture and non governmental organizations in international development policy. *Von Hoffmann* asked Dr. Wolfgang *Weiß* (Bayreuth) to explain the connection between these issues in consideration of the problems of the world trade system.

Weiß agreed that alongside governmental organizations like UNCTAD and the Bretton Woods institutions, NGOs play an important role in international development policy. They provide resources to help finding solutions for the problems of developing countries. *Weiß* then discussed in detail the problems of developing countries in exporting goods such as agricultural or service products. As the WTO ministerial conference of Cancun had shown, industrial states like the USA or the European Union were not willing to liberalize agricultural markets. However, free markets for agricultural products are very important for developing countries, as agricultural products are frequently the only products exported by these countries. Another problem arises due to the heterogeneous structure of developing countries. Whether a country can be qualified as a developing country depends on the self-estimation of that country. Therefore, a country like Singapore still counts as a developing state. Though international rules concerning developing countries are standardized and unitary it is not possible to deal with specific problems of single states.

Professor Dr. Roland *Eckert*'s (Trier) contribution referred to the sociological aspects of development policy. In his view, the history of modernization demonstrates that highly developed countries like England often protected their markets. The same protectionist tendencies can be seen today in Asian states like Korea, Japan or other so called tiger states. According to *Eckert* the world is faced with a paradoxical situation. On one hand the developing countries are demanding freedom of enterprise. On the other hand the industrial states are protecting their economies. *Eckert* asked *Weiß* how this problem could be solved. Furthermore, *Eckert* expressed his doubts about the competences of international governmental institutions to provide scientific knowledge to developing countries, because they are acting on their own interests. Here, he considered NGOs to be important actors in helping developing countries to produce the expertise they cannot produce themselves.

Weiß agreed stating that in consequence states had to give more power and competences to UNCTAD. Most members of UNCTAD are developing countries, therefore the UNCTAD offered for them more possibilities to discuss and solve the problems of international development policy.

Professor Dr. El-Shagi *El-Shagi* (Trier) did not agree with *Eckert*'s opinion about the relationship between protectionism and development. He argued that protectionism never lead to development in the past. He illustrated this by referring to the so-called tiger states. Some experts had claimed that these countries had succeeded in their development due to protectionist measures. In his opinion these countries did not develop because of protectionism but in spite of protectionism. He indicated that one could not find any economic sector in Korea that prospered because of protectionism. *El-Shagi* then asked *Weiß* to explain the term "coherence" more precisely, since he considered the term to be rather imprecise.

Weiß agreed with *El-Shagi* that free trade was in the interest of developing countries. This had now become the position of many of these countries as well. *Weiß* criticized the attitude of industrial states like the USA and the European Community to demand freedom of trade and at the same time refuse to liberalize their own markets. This "lip service" of industrial states was the reason for the failure of the WTO conference of Cancun. He mentioned that the European Community was changing its agricultural policy, but conceded that that it would take some time before results would become visible. On the issue of coherence he said that improving the position of developing countries could not be achieved by implementing legal standards into domestic law alone. It was also necessary to help developing countries to solve practical problems like establishing an effective administration. The need to take action against corruption, for instance, was an important element for incorporating the guidelines (directives) of the WTO.

El-Shagi expressed his doubts whether an effective fight against corruption in developing countries might ever be possible. He believes that no real concepts for the successful prevention of corruption are available. At the same time, he indicated, the differences between developing countries and industrialized nations regarding corruption might be smaller than assumed. The Industrial nations could not always serve as a good example for the developing countries. The rigidity of the German administration, for example, would make it hard to react quickly and effectively to crises, a point which is frequently criticized in the administrations of developing countries.

Professor Dr. Matthias *Ruffert* (Jena) mentioned the discussion on public international law, about the existence of a collective right to development. He asked *Weiß* whether he thought that this discussion had come to an end due to the development of WTO. *Weiß* replied that it was difficult to tell how such a right of development should be interpreted. It was also a very broad and imprecise concept compared to WTO rules on differential treatment. He did not see any valuable contribution from the discussion of a right to development to reshaping the rules on differential treatment.

Professor Dr. Meinhard *Schröder* (Trier) asked if aspects of environmental policy could play a role for concepts of development. He also inquired how the role of an international lawyer could be described in these concepts.

Professor Dr. Christine *Langenfeld* (Göttingen) asked for the correlation between good governance and free trade and the functioning of a just international economic system.

Professor Dr. Peter *Eigen* (Berlin) wondered if *Weiß*' analysis did not include circular phrases such as the statement that non-trade issues should not be treated by a trade organization. He stressed in contrast to *El-Shagi*'s intervention that the term "coherence" had many connotations and should not be reduced on technical issues alone. One should not limit technical assistance to helping developing countries to live up to their obligations. From his experience at the World Bank he saw tremendous working possibilities for international lawyers regardless of whether they are employed by a governmental or non-governmental organization. *Eigen* added that the WTO was one of the last organizations to realize that fighting corruption and promoting good governance are essential for economic development. He also noted that the Singapore Issues on public procurement were a very important element in free world trade. He also warned not to be too negative about the functioning of WTO in the field of development.

Weiß agreed in general but emphasized the necessity of liberalization on the part of industrial countries. He agreed that the WTO had an important role to play. In his opinion the tasks of international lawyers in the field of development policy is mainly to make international organizations work more effectively for the interests of the poor and to find solutions for concurring objectives. *Weiß* stated that environmental policy was an important aspect of development. But it had to be kept in mind that developing countries do not have unlimited resources. Therefore developing countries had to work primarily on major problems like improving the living conditions of the population. The mandate of the WTO should not be overloaded.

Olivier Frémond

FINDINGS FROM THE WORLD BANK CORPORATE GOVERNANCE COUNTRY ASSESSMENTS

I. Abstract

Corporate governance focuses on the ways in which the rights of suppliers of equity to corporations are protected in order to receive a fair return. Good practices reduce the risk of expropriation of outsiders by insiders and thus, the cost of capital for issuers. *Capaul and Frémond* review the findings of 28 corporate governance country assessments conducted in the developing countries and transition economies of Eastern and Central Europe, Latin America, Africa, East Asia and South Asia prepared under the joint World Bank/International Monetary Fund initiatives of the "Reports on the Observance of Standards and Codes" (ROSCs) and "Financial Sector Assessment Program" (FSAP). Using the OECD Principles of Corporate Governance as a benchmark, the assessments, which were conducted between 2000 and 2003, focus on the rights of shareholders, the equitable treatment of shareholders, the role of stakeholders, disclosure and transparency, and the duties of the board of directors of listed companies. This paper, which updates "The State of Corporate Governance: Experience from Country Assessments," published by the authors in June 2002, gives an overview of the continuing contributions of the assessments to policy dialogue, World Bank diagnostic and strategic work and lending and non-lending operations, and presents the unfinished agenda.

This paper reviews the experience and insights gained from the preparation of 28 corporate governance country assessments[1] across Latin America, Asia, Europe and Africa and updates "The State of Corporate Governance: Experience from Country Assessments," published in June 2002.[2] These assessments were conducted between 2000 and 2003 under the joint IMF/World Bank "Reports on the Observance of Standards and Codes" (ROSC) and "Financial Sector Assessment Program" (FSAP) initiatives. The assessments focus on the rights of shareholders, the equitable treatment of shareholders, the role of

---

1 Brazil (initial plus update), Bulgaria, Chile, Colombia, Croatia, Czech Republic (initial plus update), Egypt, Georgia, Hong Kong, Hungary, India, Korea, Latvia, Lithuania, Malaysia, Mauritius, Mexico, Morocco, Philippines, Poland, Romania, South Africa, Slovakia, Turkey, Ukraine, Zimbabwe.

2 *Frémond, O./Capaul, M.*, "The State of Corporate Governance: Experience from Country Assessments," The World Bank Group, Working Paper 2858, 2002.

stakeholders, disclosure and transparency, and the duties of the board of listed companies. Section I summarizes the origins and objectives of the FSAP and ROSC programs. Section II reviews the Organization for Economic Co-Operation and Development (OECD) Principles of Corporate Governance, the standard against which countries are benchmarked, and focuses on the assessments themselves. A discussion of the reports, including an analysis of the framework of the policy recommendations and a summary of key findings, is also presented. Section III gives an overview of the assessments' actual and potential contributions to policy dialogue, diagnostic and strategic work, lending and non-lending operations – which can be carried out by international financial institutions, bilaterals, policymakers, and the private sector. Section IV presents the unfinished agenda.

Corporate governance is about the definition of property rights of shareholders and the mechanisms for exercising them. Equity rights are complex property rights. The right to participate in company profits depends on a company's ability to generate a profit and on how profits will be distributed. Corporate governance focuses on the ways in which the rights of suppliers of equity to firms are protected and receive a fair return.[3] Good corporate governance practices reduce the risk of expropriation of outsiders by insiders and the cost of capital for issuers and countries. Corporate governance also deals with the market for corporate control. Property rights must be well established and defined for this market to function efficiently.

Empirical evidence suggests that good corporate governance increases the efficiency of capital allocation within and across firms, reduces the cost of capital, helps broaden access to capital, reduces vulnerability to crises, fosters savings provisions, and renders corruption more difficult.

The World Bank's corporate governance country assessments are a diagnostic instrument. They assess the laws, rules, regulations and practices of listed companies and investors in a country. They are most relevant to middle income countries, but are also a useful tool for transition economies, where mass privatization has created many listed firms with thousands of shareholders, and for low-income countries seeking to attract capital for growth. The assessments do not advocate a single model of corporate governance; rather, they promote choice for issuers, investors and policymakers.

The key findings of this paper are:

---

3 *Shleifer, A./Vishny, R. W.*, "A Survey of Corporate Governance," *The Journal of Finance*, Volume LII, Issue 2, June 1997.

- There is now wide acceptance of the importance of corporate governance reform and of the value of the OECD Principles. Recent scandals in the U.S. and elsewhere have further reinforced this trend. Corporate governance reforms are underway in almost every country surveyed.
- At the same time, a number of factors are holding back reform. Market declines in many countries over the past few years have reduced investor interest (particularly foreign investor interest) in emerging equity markets. In some countries, a certain amount of "reform fatigue" has resulted from frequent changes in corporate governance rules and provisions.
- In most countries, reforms are only just beginning to penetrate the business culture. Change will be slow and gradual.
- None of the assessed countries comply with the OECD Principles in all respects. Yet all countries surveyed have undertaken or are undertaking reforms to bring their legal and regulatory frameworks in compliance with the Principles. Moreover, as of January 2003, over 43 countries had developed their own corporate governance codes of best practice. The World Bank corporate governance assessments have triggered interest and reform.
- Generally, there is a discrepancy between the letter of the law and actual practices. The enforcement of shareholders rights and equitable treatment of shareholders consistently need strengthening. In most assessed countries, business transactions have traditionally taken place on the basis of relationships and trust; little attention has been paid to publicly available information. Corporate governance reform is a way to extend this trust to all market participants.
- The OECD Principles assume that countries have an efficient legal and regulatory framework in place and that securities regulators have the means and ability to enforce their capital markets' rules and regulations. Experience shows that this is often not the case. Typically, courts are under-financed, unmotivated, unclear as to how the law applies, unfamiliar with economic issues, or even corrupt. In weak regulatory environments, concentrated enforcement through the market regulators may be preferable to enforcement through the courts. Securities regulators, however, do not have enough direct power to enforce penalties. Enforcement of prevailing rules and regulations falls largely to the courts. The result is poor enforcement of the rules and regulations underlying corporate governance.
- A "menu of options" approach to corporate governance standards provides a means for issuers and investors to choose the markets and com-

panies most appropriate to their risk profile. At the same time, standardization of options is desirable to lower transaction costs for issuers and investors. Choice in the form of different corporate governance options offered to issuers is therefore an effective mechanism to facilitate reform.

II. The ROSC/FSAP Initiatives

1. The role of standards in the international financial architecture

In the wake of the international financial crisis of the 1990s, the international community undertook a range of initiatives to strengthen the international financial architecture through crisis prevention, mitigation and resolution. The agenda focused on weaknesses in the international financial system that could lead to or exacerbate global instability, hence requiring collective action at the international level.

There is broad consensus that global financial stability depends on robust national systems and, therefore, requires enhanced country-level measures. Given the integration of capital markets, national financial crises can imperil international financial stability. This provides a basic "public goods" rationale for minimum standards that benefit international and national systems.

The Financial Stability Forum, the G7, G20 and G22[4] have emphasized the role of minimum standards and codes in strengthening the international financial architecture. Standards enhance transparency, identify elements that may contribute to economic and financial vulnerability, and foster market efficiency and discipline. At the national level, standards provide a benchmark to identify weaknesses and guide policy reform. To serve these aims, the scope and application of such standards must be reviewed in the context of a country's overall development strategy and tailored to individual country conditions. The IMF and World Bank are assessing the observance of 12 core standards relevant to private and financial sector development and macroeconomic stability in systemically important countries and other World Bank client nations.[5]

---

4 G7: Canada, France, Germany, Italy, Japan, UK, U.S. G20: G7 plus Argentina, Australia, Brazil, China, India, Indonesia, Korea, Mexico, Russia, Saudi Arabia, South Africa, Turkey, EU. IMF and World Bank participate in the discussions. G22: G7 plus Argentina, Australia, Brazil, China, Hong Kong SAR, India, Indonesia, Korea, Malaysia, Mexico, Poland, Russia, Singapore, South Africa, Thailand.

5 The full list of the 12 standards is set out in Annex A.

The Bretton Woods institutions have formed a joint initiative called the "Reports on the Observance of Standards and Codes" (ROSCs). The IMF takes the lead in preparing assessments covering data dissemination and fiscal transparency. Modules for the financial sector (monetary and financial policy transparency, banking supervision, securities market regulation, payment systems, deposit insurance) are mostly derived from the Financial Sector Assessment Program (FSAP). The World Bank takes the lead in three areas:

(i) corporate governance,

(ii) accounting and auditing, and

(iii) insolvency regimes and creditor rights.

2. *ROSC and FSAP assessments*

The ROSC and FSAP programs assess financial sector vulnerability and development needs. They provide input to the IMF for its surveillance activities and are useful tools to support the policy dialogue of international financial institutions, policymakers and the private sector. They contribute to the design of loans and preparation of key policy documents and provide benchmarks for the design and monitoring of technical assistance and capacity building.

Countries voluntarily participate in a ROSC or FSAP, or both. The FSAP contains a section that remains confidential between the Fund/Bank and the assessed country. In contrast, ROSC assessments are intended as public documents. The IMF and World Bank have set up websites to disseminate ROSC assessments for the benefit of country authorities, investors and other interested parties. The completed assessments are submitted to country authorities for review and published if authorities voice no objections. Countries may deny publication or reserve a "right of reply," whereby their unresolved objections are published with the assessment. The utility of the assessments increases with periodic updates that show progress over time.[6]

III. The World Bank Corporate Governance Assessments

The first step in developing a methodology to assess a country's corporate governance system was the identification of a standard. The World Bank selected the OECD Principles of Corporate Governance as the standard. The OECD Principles were agreed upon by a large number of countries (29) of varied legal, economic and cultural traditions and after extensive consultation

6 Second ROSCs have been completed or are underway for Brazil, the Czech Republic, Egypt, India and Poland.

with the World Bank, the IMF, the Bank of International Settlements, and representatives of the business community from Japan, Germany, France, UK and the U.S., as well as emerging market governments, international investors, trade unions and other interested parties. As such, the OECD Principles represent the minimum standard that countries with different traditions could agree upon, without being unduly prescriptive. They are equally applicable to countries with civil and common law traditions, different levels of ownership concentration, and various models of board representation.

1. The benchmark: the OECD principles of corporate governance

The OECD Principles of Corporate Governance are general guidelines for regulating the entry, on-going obligations, and exit of companies to and from equities markets. The Principles were devised with the key concepts of responsibility, accountability, fairness and transparency in mind and allow for diversity of rules and regulations.

The OECD Principles are primarily concerned with listed companies. They are organized into five sections:

(1) the rights of shareholders;

(2) the equitable treatment of shareholders;

(3) the role of stakeholders in corporate governance;

(4) disclosure and transparency, and

(5) the responsibilities of the board.

The International Organization of Securities Commissions (IOSCO) Principles of Financial Market Regulation address regulators of financial markets, self-regulating organizations, enforcement, cooperation in regulation, collective investment schemes (investment funds), market intermediaries, secondary securities markets and issuers. In 2002, IOSCO endorsed the OECD Principles, recommending that its members "foster good corporate governance through legislation, regulations and codes of good practice using the OECD Principles as a benchmark."

The OECD Principles state that board members are accountable to shareholders and to the company.[7] Accountability to shareholders means equal treatment of majority and minority shareholders. Accountability to the company means that directors must ensure that the company complies with existing laws and regulations, such as tax, labor, health and safety laws, equal opportunity, environmental legislation, and competition law.

7 Source: Preface to the OECD Principles.

The Principles stress that stakeholders, especially creditors, employees and consumers, play an integral part in shaping company decisions. Principle III states that "...the corporate governance framework should encourage active co-operation between corporations and stakeholders in creating wealth, jobs and the sustainability of financially sound enterprises." The full social responsibility debate, however, extends beyond the scope of this paper.

Corporate governance deals with the checks and balances that must exist to address problems arising from the separation of corporate management and ownership. Board members and management need enough independence to manage company affairs as they see fit without undue interference from outsiders, as long as they do it prudently, with diligence and care, and in the interests of shareholders. Checks and balances are needed to ensure accountability, since people are likely to manage their own affairs more carefully than those of others.

The OECD Principles are non-binding. They provide a framework for dialogue on country experience and identification of policy reform "without prejudice to the prerogative of each nation to find its own path to better corporate governance."[8] The aim is a common framework under which good practices can develop, in consistency with national regulations and traditions.[9]

A consultation process is currently underway to assess the effectiveness of the OECD Principles as a policy tool and core standard. Since they were drafted, there has been growing discussion with respect to potential gaps in the Principles and the possible need for more specific guidance, rather than simply general principles. The question has also arisen as to whether different standards are needed for countries at different stages of development. The Principles were scheduled for re-assessment in 2005, but U.S. and other corporate scandals in 2001/2002 led to the decision to accelerate the process. Preparatory work began in 2002, and the update is expected to be completed in 2003/2004. The first stage included a survey of major corporate governance developments and emerging issues around the world, based in part on a questionnaire circulated to OECD member countries.[10] A meeting of the OECD Steering Group on Corporate Governance in June 2003 focused discussion on the survey's

---

8 Source:OECD Principles.

9 *Ibid.*

10 The 30 OECD members are: Australia, Austria, Belgium, Canada, Czech Republic, Denmark, Finland, France, Germany, Greece, Hungary, Iceland, Ireland, Italy, Japan, Korea, Luxembourg, Mexico, Norway, New Zealand, Netherlands, Poland, Portugal, Slovak Republic, Spain, Sweden, Switzerland, Turkey, United Kingdom, and the United States.

results and sought views toward establishing a consensus on changes to the Principles in light of lessons learned since their inception. The Steering Group's next meeting will take place in November 2003.

Since the Principles were implemented, several new codes have been released, including the Combined Code in the UK, the International Institute of Finance's Policies for Corporate Governance and Transparency for Emerging Markets, and the King II Report in South Africa. These are, in some respects, more prescriptive than the OECD Principles.

The Regional Roundtables on Corporate Governance, a joint OECD/World Bank initiative, follow the structure of the five sections of the OECD Principles. The Roundtables were launched by the Memorandum of Understanding signed by World Bank President *J. Wolfensohn* and OECD Secretary General *D. Johnston* in June 1999 to disseminate best practice in corporate governance and increase the ownership of reform in developing countries and transition economies. In addition, the World Bank and the OECD set up the Global Corporate Governance Forum, a multi-donor trust fund, to

(a) disseminate best practice and raise awareness of the need for reform;

(b) foster academic research; and

(c) provide a source of finance for implementation of reform and capacity building.[11]

2. *Process and format*

a) *The Template*

To assess countries, the World Bank produced a questionnaire (the "Template"), structured along the five chapters of the OECD Principles. Its aim is to facilitate the collection of information necessary for a diagnostic of the institutional framework underlying corporate governance, as well as prevailing practices and enforcement. For each OECD Principle, a set of questions has been prepared to assess the compliance of a given country. Most questions have been drafted to yield "yes" or "no" responses in order to facilitate benchmarking.[12]

---

11 For more information on the Global Corporate Governance Forum, please visit www.gcgf.org.

12 The Corporate Governance Template is posted at http://www.worldbank.org/ifa/rosc_cg.html.

The Template includes a section on country ownership structure, a key determinant of corporate governance practices. It seeks to identify pyramid structures, crossholdings, business groups and the divergence between cash flow and voting rights. While the OECD Principles are concerned with shareholder and stakeholder rights, disclosure and the responsibilities of insiders, the Template also addresses the issue of institutional capacity.

A first Template was produced in 2000 and was revised in 2001 and 2003 in consultation with World Bank and international experts.[13] Originally, the Template was applicable mainly to non-financial enterprises. The current, third generation Template consists of a main section that focuses on listed, non-financial firms, with separate, special pilot modules to assess banks and non-banking financial institutions, i.e. insurance companies, pension funds and mutual funds.[14] This third generation Template, enhanced through the experience gained in conducting more than two dozen assessments, also includes more detailed questions on the governance of securities regulators in a manner complementary to the IOSCO Principles.

Information collected from the Template questionnaires for each country is also being compiled into a database of corporate governance indicators, which will permit the generation of a "snapshot" of each country's corporate governance framework, as well the systematic comparison of frameworks.

b) The assessment

Corporate governance country assessments may be conducted as assisted self-assessments. Under an assisted self-assessment, the country is involved in all stages of the process. This approach works well when country authorities are committed to reform. In the assisted self-assessment, the ability of local authorities to provide objective and complete information may be impaired by political considerations. For example, it may be hard for a regulator to acknowledge that existing laws are not always well-enforced. On the other hand, the assisted self-assessment increases the degree of ownership of domestic policymakers and helps develop capacity.

---

13 Corporate governance experts from the World Bank Group, OECD, IMF, Commonwealth Association, U.S. Securities Commission, King Commission, as well as private sector experts of corporate governance from industrialized and developing countries, were asked to provide guidance and opinions.

14 Several assessments of financial institutions are underway, but these modules are beyond the scope of this paper.

The assessment format facilitates systematic benchmarking across countries and regions. It is divided into four parts:

(i) executive summary;

(ii) capital market overview and institutional framework;

(iii) principle by principle review, including policy recommendations and,

(iv) summary of recommendations highlighting areas for legislative reform, institutional strengthening and voluntary/private initiatives.

The assessments attempt to differentiate between compliance of the legal and regulatory framework and actual practices of market participants, and include a chapter on institutional strengthening. Hence, each OECD Principle is evaluated according to quantitative and qualitative standards. "Observed" means that all essential criteria are met. "Largely observed" means that only minor shortcomings are observed, which do not raise any questions about the authorities' ability and intent to achieve full observance within a reasonable period of time. "Partially observed" means that while the legal and regulatory framework may be fully compliant with the OECD Principle, practices and enforcement diverge. "Materially not observed" means that, despite progress, shortcomings are sufficient to raise doubts about the authorities' ability to achieve observance. "Not observed" means that no substantive progress toward observance has been achieved.

The assessment is most useful when the assessed country is committed to a reform agenda and agrees to the report's publication on the ROSC website at http://www.worldbank.org/ifa/rosc_cg.html.

The assessments complement private sector rating activities. The Bank assessments focus on country analysis, while most rating agencies focus on companies. Standard & Poor's and Moody's rate firms in emerging markets. Similar exercises are carried out by specialized firms, such as Pensions Investment Research Consultants in the UK and Deminor in Belgium and France. Rating companies for corporate governance have emerged in Russia and Korea. Other organizations that have generated country-level analyses include the OECD, European Bank for Reconstruction and Development (EBRD), the Institute of International Finance (IIF), the Asian Development Bank (ADB), CLSA Emerging Markets and Davis Global Advisors.

3. ***Policy recommendations***

In the global market, both countries and issuers compete for capital. Policy recommendations are suggestions for countries that want to compete for international portfolio capital. A "one size fits all" solution is not advocated. The recommendations may include examples of how other countries have overcome similar problems. They provide choice for issuers, countries and investors. The driving principle is to encourage choice and let market forces pick the winners.

Choice enables reputational costs and benefits to play their role. Without choice, the benefit of complying with international best practice is difficult to capture. Choice allows issuers to signal to the market that they are different. Already, Brazil's *Novo Mercado* sets the standards for companies wishing to issue capital. Over time, it is expected that governance regimes that are less transparent and provide less protection to minority investors, will find it more difficult and expensive to attract capital.

The policy recommendations offer different options for compliance with the OECD Principles. Recommendations may include changes to existing laws or rules or the adoption of new ones. They also focus on how companies can improve their internal governance structures. Endorsement and ownership of the reform program by the private sector is essential for successful corporate governance reform. Therefore, recommendations may include measures to encourage the development of private sector associations, such as institutes of directors, not-for-profit shareholder associations or other business associations, which operate in parallel with existing public institutions and provide private solutions to information dissemination.

The policy recommendations should be construed as a set of interdependent measures that must be implemented to be most effective. For example, one way of enhancing the equitable treatment of shareholders is through cumulative voting[15] for the election of board members, so that minority shareholders have a chance for board representation. This measure alone, however, may not be effective. For example, the introduction of cumulative voting in the Philippines did not result in greater representation of minority shareholders on boards, because often, too few minority shareholders attended and voted at the annual general meeting (AGM) to win enough votes for one candidate. Com-

---

15 Cumulative voting allows minority shareholders to cast all their votes for a single candidate. Suppose that a listed firm has two shareholders, one holding 80 percent of the votes and another with 20 percent. Five board members must be elected this year. Without a cumulative voting rule, each shareholder must vote separately for each position. The majority shareholder will prevail for all five seats, since s/he will outvote the minority shareholder each time by 80:20. With cumulative voting in place, the minority shareholder can decide how to place his/her votes. The optimal strategy for him/her would be to cast all his/her votes (5 times 20 percent) for one board member. The minority shareholder will then win that seat, since s/he will have 100 percent.

plementary measures, such as proxy voting, voting by mail and the introduction of the concept of independent directors, are necessary to enhance equitable treatment. Each country's specific conditions, priorities, and level of development should drive the sequencing of reform.

4. *Key findings*

For ease of reference, the discussion of key findings is organized to correspond with the five sections of the OECD Principles. Each section highlights deviations from the Principles or describes compliance. One key finding is that although the legal and regulatory frameworks of the assessed countries are approaching compliance with the OECD Principles, practices are not. The challenge of the assessments is to reflect the discrepancies between the letter of the law and compliance. Annex D sets out a matrix showing the overall areas of compliance and deviation from the benchmark among the surveyed countries.[16]

a) Section I: the rights of shareholders

Basic shareholder rights are improving in almost all countries surveyed. Shareholder record keeping infrastructure is advancing rapidly, as more countries acquire international-standard central depositories and share registries. In many countries, fundamental abuses related to shareholder meeting mechanics have been controlled through changes to the law. The relative powers of the board and shareholders are being clarified. However, a number of items of interest to international investors remain unresolved in many countries (especially share blocking requirements and short meeting notification periods), and in many countries many fundamental decisions (especially large transactions or sales of assets) can be taken by the board without any shareholder approval.

Registration of shares has historically been the company's responsibility. Vesting this power in management created difficulties stemming from agency problems between managers and shareholders. In some countries, such as Croatia, Morocco, Turkey and Mauritius, companies can block share transfer and ownership registration. In India, the transfer of physical shares often results in delays and increases the likelihood of fraud or theft. Such practices impair the right of shareholders to secure ownership registration. Most countries surveyed have created central depositories that speed up the process of

16 Annex D shows findings for the 20 countries whose ROSCs have been approved for public dissemination.

share transfer and registration and make them more secure. This removes the power to register shares from insiders.

While voting is a basic right of ordinary shares in most countries, owners of bearer shares may not vote in Egypt. In Brazil, the majority of investors own shares without voting rights (the so-called PN shares[17]). On the other hand, shareholders who have paid up only 50 percent of the share issue price have full voting rights in Croatia, Morocco and Egypt.

In most assessed countries, fundamental corporate decisions are made with a supermajority – usually 67 or 75 percent – of shares voting and present. Exceptions include Romania, Turkey, Brazil, Colombia and Mexico, where a simple majority is sufficient to pass many, if not all, decisions.

In most countries, shareholders can delegate the authority to issue new shares to the board. This does not contradict the OECD Principles. However, in some countries, this practice is abused. In Croatia, companies may receive authorization from shareholders (if approved by 75 percent of shares at the meeting) to issue up to 50 percent of share capital for a period of up to five years. The law also allows the management board to increase the company's share capital by converting company bonds into new shares up to the amount of the share capital of the company. In addition, the law permits company statutes to waive existing shareholders' pre-emptive rights on new share issues (also the case in Lithuania, Colombia, the Czech Republic, and Georgia, albeit with the approval of a supermajority of shareholders).

There is evidence that policymakers in many jurisdictions are recognizing the importance of strengthening minority shareholder rights by lowering the percentage of capital or voting rights necessary to initiate corporate actions. As recommended under the OECD Principles, shareholders owning 5 or 10 percent of capital can convene a shareholder meeting in most countries surveyed.[18] Before 2001, it took 33 percent of capital to call a shareholders meeting in Mexico; now 10 percent of voting or limited voting capital may do so. Some countries have provisions that permit shareholders to add items to the AGM agenda. This right may have deadlines or other restrictions attached. In Hong Kong, for example, shareholders representing 5 percent of capital or 100 shareholders owning an average of HK $2,000 of par value may add items; however, they must, as in most of the surveyed countries that allow such an

17 Non-voting PN shares can constitute up to 2/3 of total share capital. The new corporate law lowers this limit to 50 percent for new companies and new share offerings.

18 In Korea and the Czech Republic, as few as 3 percent can call a meeting, while in Colombia, the requirement remains an exceptionally high 20 percent.

addition, circulate the new agenda at their own expense. In Bulgaria, shareholders may only add items prior to the agenda's publication in the press. In Croatia, shareholders have until ten days after publication to add, change or counter-propose items; however, these are not circulated to the other shareholders. In some countries, like Colombia, a detailed agenda is not circulated, so shareholders do not have an opportunity to add items.

On voting procedures and the right to vote in absentia, all countries allow physical proxies. About 1/3 of the countries assessed permit voting by mail, while none, with the exception of Colombia, have electronic voting.[19] India, for example, allows postal voting for some important resolutions such as mergers and acquisitions and buy-back of shares. Korea also permits voting by mail, although few Korean firms have adopted this provision in their statutes. In Colombia, electronic and postal voting are allowed, but decisions are valid only if 100 percent of shareholders vote.

On paper, disclosure of capital structures is generally in line with the OECD Principles. Typically, the annual report, stock exchange, registrar or the AGM provide information on the first level of ownership beyond the 5 or 10 percent threshold. Strictly speaking, therefore, most countries comply with the OECD Principle. However, if there are pyramid structures and cross shareholdings, or nominee owners, it is difficult to identify ultimate controlling shareholders. In some countries, such as Romania, investors often protect themselves behind off-shore vehicles where ownership disclosure is not required.

The assessed countries are largely characterized by concentrated ownership structures. Ownership concentration implies that only friendly corporate takeovers are possible. Malaysia, Poland and India, for example, have takeover regulations that include mandatory tender offer rules. In Chile, the threshold triggering an offer for all outstanding shares is 67 percent. In Egypt, Mexico and Colombia, the offer does not extend to all shares. In Korea, anyone who intends to acquire 5 percent or more of the shares from ten shareholders outside the stock market must undertake a formal tender offer.

Concerning the OECD Principle that states that shareholders should consider the costs and benefits of exercising their voting rights, in most countries surveyed, there is little shareholder culture, and the costs of exercising voting rights and the danger of upsetting management are seen to outweigh the benefits in the short run. However, some countries, like Malaysia and some of the Latin American countries like Brazil, are taking steps in this direction. Also, in

---

19 Countries that allow postal ballots include Croatia, Colombia, Georgia, Hong Kong, Hungary, Korea, Lithuania, Mauritius and Zimbabwe.

many countries, pension funds are not well developed (In some countries, such as in Latin America, pension funds are becoming increasingly powerful; however, they sometimes do not invest or are prohibited from investing in equities, as is the case in Mexico). However, it can be argued that this OECD Principle is more important in developing and transition economies than in industrialized ones, because in the latter, investors can "vote with their feet," i.e. sell their shares if they are dissatisfied with the governance of their portfolio firms. In the former, investors cannot do so easily without moving the market. Most countries surveyed require that shares be blocked from trading for a certain time before the AGM, except for Romania, which has a "date of record." A date of record for proof of ownership creates incentives for institutional investors to vote, because it does not inhibit them from selling their shares after the date of record.

b) Section II: the equitable treatment of shareholders

The assessments reveal that more and more emphasis is being placed on shareholder redress and enforcement to improve the equitable treatment of shareholders. As mentioned above, in many countries there are lowered thresholds for shareholder action, and regulators and exchanges have become more active in trying to enforce the law. However, the results of basic legal reform have sometimes been disappointing. Many new laws have not been used much in practice. Enforcement remains the key challenge.

The concept of minority shareholder protection is especially important in countries where ownership is concentrated; however, the concept is underdeveloped in the countries surveyed. Most countries comply with the requirement that shareholders should have timely and sufficient information about the AGM, although in Georgia, Brazil, the Philippines, Mauritius, Colombia and Mexico, the notice periods are too short,[20] agendas are not well-circulated and important agenda items can be omitted. In India and the Czech Republic, some firms hold the AGM in remote places, making it hard and often expensive for minority shareholders to attend.[21] With regard to the exercise of voting rights by custodians or nominees in agreement with beneficial owners, it is impossible to track beneficial owners in Croatia, Georgia and the Philippines, while in Egypt the concept has recently been introduced in the Depository Law.

---

20 Generally deemed to be less than 20-30 days. Ukraine's 45-day notice requirement stands out as particularly generous.

21 Mauritius stands out as an interesting example, as companies are not held liable for failing to give notice of meetings in the case of an "accidental" omission.

Despite the fact that insider trading and self-dealing are or are in the process of becoming criminal offenses in all assessed countries, monitoring and detection remain a problem across the board. Securities regulators are generally ill-equipped to carry out surveillance activities efficiently, and they depend on an often overburdened, weak or slow court system for enforcement. In addition, commercial tribunals are rare.

Disclosure by directors and managers of material interests in transactions or matters affecting the company is less than fully observed in most countries. The regulatory framework usually includes rules and regulations for disclosing and monitoring related party transactions and self-dealing. However, disclosure is not always mandatory, and there are often no clear rules. There is a general concern that existing provisions are not consistently adhered to and cannot be enforced in environments often characterized by pyramid structures, cross shareholdings and a weak judicial system. In contrast, Chile stands out, certainly in Latin America, as being progressive in this area; shareholders representing 5 percent of capital may request that a related party transaction be approved with a 2/3 majority.

c) Section III: the role of stakeholders

Stakeholders are defined as all those who have a material relationship with the company not necessarily based on share ownership. These include employees, creditors, customers, suppliers, local communities, and society as a whole. The OECD Principles state that the corporate governance framework should recognize the rights of stakeholders as established by law and encourage active cooperation between corporations and stakeholders in creating wealth, jobs, and the sustainability of financially sound enterprises.

Stakeholders are protected by contracts, competitive markets and through laws and regulation. Regulation is essential, because markets are imperfect. Sometimes, laws generate negative externalities or fail to protect stakeholders adequately. For example, contract law cannot govern all aspects of employee-firm relationship. Therefore, the law of labor contracting, pension law, health and safety law, and anti-discrimination law have been developed. Similarly, firms may have an incentive to conduct activities that may damage the environment of nearby communities. Therefore, environmental legislation and the law of nuisance and mass tort are necessary. Likewise, product safety regulation, warranty law, tort law governing product liability, antitrust law, and mandatory disclosure of product content protect consumers. Other rules and regulations include tax, bankruptcy, corporate and securities laws. These laws are needed to protect the interests of states, creditors and minority investors. For example, corporate and bankruptcy laws protect creditors from shareholder abuses. Modern corporate law includes rules for "piercing the corporate veil," whereby creditors can hold shareholders liable beyond their limited liability when the latter's interference in company affairs makes a company unable to service its debts. Similarly, creditors can block dividend distribution in the presence of inadequate capital.[22]

To comply with the OECD Principles, boards must put in place adequate mechanisms and procedures to familiarize their members with existing legislation related to stakeholder rights. Companies also need to consult and communicate with employees and other stakeholders.

While such legal and regulatory frameworks may exist in developing countries and transition economies, the lack of judiciary enforcement capability often results in insufficient stakeholder protection. When this is the case, additional protections – like board representation – may be warranted. In addition, some companies have found it advantageous to take voluntary measures to foster good stakeholder relations. In India, for example, some top listed companies have put in place various internal and control mechanisms on their own initiative; IT giant Infosys recently implemented a whistle-blower policy.

Worldwide, stakeholders are seldom represented on the board. Exceptions are Egypt and countries in the ECA region, like the Czech Republic and Hungary, where employees have the right to elect representatives to the (supervisory) board. In transition economies, such as Poland, it is customary for creditors to sit on the board of the company to whom they lend. Their interest is thus protected by board representation. At Slovakian firms with over 50 employees, employees may elect 1/3 of supervisory board members.

The debate in transition economies on the role of stakeholders in corporate governance has been developing in a different context from the one prevailing in OECD economies and developing countries. The main concern of transition has been to move away from the model of the enterprise as a social unit toward that of an enterprise that is a profit-making entity based on clear property rights and capable of attracting capital.

In Romania, unions have a voice in corporate restructurings and collective bargaining. Employees have a right to be informed by companies and to conduct negotiations through employee representatives in cases of an increase in capital, a reorganization, a liquidation and other key decisions that might impact on workers' conditions. Trade unions can also initiate consultations. In many of the assessed countries, consultation and other labor rights contained

22 Insolvency and Creditor Rights ROSCs deal with this topic in greater depth.

in labor laws are not always observed in practice. In Colombia, employees are considered to be company creditors and enjoy similar rights in restructuring.

Bondholders are the stakeholder group that tends to be recognized in the legal framework and have access to relevant information, including the right to send a representative to the AGM (Annual General Meeting of Shareholders). Although not widespread in practice, share options and profit-sharing schemes are permitted in many countries. However, their structure does not always align the interests of managers and employees with shareholders. In Morocco, for example, they have been issued at a discount to prevailing market price. Thus, the incentive for managers to improve performance and increase share price is significantly reduced.

d) Section IV: disclosure and transparency

In most countries surveyed, considerable emphasis has been placed on improving transparency through financial and non-financial disclosure. In general, in almost every country surveyed, there are greatly improved disclosure rules, standards, and formats. The items required in statutory reports, and their required frequency and timeliness, have increased. At the same time, accounting and auditing reform is gradually moving ahead, pushed by the adoption of the Sarbanes-Oxley-Act in the U.S. The concept of audit committee is now standard in many countries and is expected to improve audit independence. Electronic information dissemination is now increasingly standard. However, compliance with new rules is growing more slowly, and the quality of financial reporting remains mixed in many countries.

Ownership and related party transaction disclosure are two key elements of the overall disclosure framework that are vital from a corporate governance perspective. The basic rules have been put in place in many countries. However, the compliance with ownership and related party transaction disclosure rules remains very spotty in many countries. Understanding the ultimate ownership structure of many large companies in emerging markets remains difficult.

Material information should be available to investors to formulate a rational investment decision. Improving the disclosure of material information provides investors with information to adjust their risk/reward perception. Incentives shape the approach to information disclosure. In countries where business has traditionally been based on relationship and trust, corporate information is often considered secret; and it is accepted practice to keep different sets of books for taxes, outside investors, and the majority shareholder.

According to the OECD Principles, information should be disseminated in a fair, timely and cost effective manner. All of the countries surveyed only partially comply with international financial reporting standards. The assessments follow the recommendation of the Financial Stability Forum and use the International Accounting (IAS) and Auditing Standards (ISA) as benchmarks.[23] Companies in Morocco and Egypt limit themselves to the publication of summary financial statements (sometimes with partial notes) in the newspaper or legal gazette.

Material information includes financial and non-financial information. Non-financial information includes:

(i) company objectives;

(ii) off balance sheet commitments and litigation risks;

(iii) the ownership structure of the company;

(iv) the remuneration of board members and key executives;

(v) material foreseeable risk factors;

(vi) material issues regarding employees and other stakeholders, and

(vii) information on governance structures and policies.

Disclosure of non-financial information is a new concept in most developing countries and transition economies. However, some progress has been recorded. For example, in Turkey, layoffs of more than 20 percent of the workforce, as well as collective bargaining agreements, must be disclosed. Malaysia and India require the disclosure of governance structures and policies under the listing rules as part of their codes of best practice. The remuneration of board members and key executives is generally set by the AGM in the aggregate. South Africa followed a gradual approach in disclosure of board remuneration. The first King report, published in 1999, recommended that aggregate compensation be disclosed in the annual report of listed companies. The second King report, released in July 2001, calls for the disclosure of individual compensation. In Bulgaria, the company prospectus for IPOs (Initial Public Offering) must disclose individual remuneration, and the Hong Kong Stock Exchange is amending its rules to require the disclosure of individual (albeit anonymous) compensation.

---

23 For further information, see the Accounting and Auditing ROSCs. Accounting and Auditing ROSCs have been published for Bulgaria, the Czech Republic, Croatia, Egypt, Kenya, Lithuania, Mauritius, Morocco, Philippines, Poland, Slovakia, South Africa and the Ukraine and deal with this topic in greater depth.

Another set of issues relates to audit practices and the legal liability of auditors. The OECD Principles remain general on this point. In most of the countries surveyed, the legal and regulatory framework delegates the setting of accounting and auditing standards to the accounting association. Compliance is generally monitored by the securities regulator or, as in South Africa, by the stock exchange. Often these institutions lack the expertise to fulfill this obligation. The professional accounting and auditing bodies are in charge of monitoring members and their professional conduct. Generally, however, monitoring is carried out by the same market practitioners that are being supervised. Also, professional associations often lack the means to impose effective sanctions. One notable exception to this rule is Morocco, although this is currently the subject of a dispute. On occasion, auditors have given unqualified opinions and certified that the accounts audited provide a fair and true picture, despite the fact that many defects were noted. The penalties for such behavior are low and enforcement generally lax. None of the countries surveyed have opted to set auditor liabilities at a high enough percentage of share capital to act as an effective deterrent.

While, in theory, most regulatory and legislative frameworks contain provisions defining auditor independence, auditors are often not perceived as such.[24] In the aftermath of Enron and other U.S. scandals,[25] it is likely that full disclosure of audit and all other fees paid to the audit firm will be adopted by a growing number of countries.

e) Section V: responsibilities of the board

Reforms to the board of directors have been a key element of corporate governance reform in most countries surveyed. There is now wide acceptance of the idea of placing more responsibility on the board, and of clarifying its role and responsibilities. Many codes of best practice focus on the board. As a result, in most countries, the board's role has been strengthened and its duties better described in law. The idea of "independence" has been introduced in many countries. Many efforts are now underway to improve director training.

---

24 Independence signifies the absence of direct or indirect personal and business relationships, past or current, between the audit firm, its partners, the company, its directors and all related parties.

25 In the fall of 2001, Enron, the U.S. energy trading company, filed for protection from creditors under Chapter 11. With the collaboration of its auditor, Arthur Andersen, Enron had used off balance sheet subsidiaries to hide the magnitude of its debts, thereby preventing shareholders from gaining a full and fair picture of the company's financial situation before it was too late.

However, true independence remains rare. There are many countries where fundamental decisions can be still be taken by board. Most director training is in early stages.

In most developing and transition economies surveyed, regardless of their legal system, companies tend to follow a "parliamentarian model" of board representation, where directors represent the constituency that elected them. This model is inconsistent with the OECD Principles. In practice, this means that boards are dominated by controllers. Policymakers across Latin America, for example, have taken two broad approaches to deal with this problem: they have mandated a minimum percentage of independent directors on the board, or, alternatively, introduced "proportional representation," which gives shareholders with a certain fixed percentage of shares the right to appoint a board member. This is the case in Brazil, where shareholders representing 15 percent of voting capital have the right to elect one board member. Starting in 2006, holders of 10 percent of non-voting shares will also elect a director.[26] In the interim, they choose one of three candidates proposed by the controller. In Colombia, board members are elected through the "electoral quotient" system. The system was devised to provide a degree of proportional representation on Colombian boards and protect minority shareholders. However, in practice, minority shareholders seldom succeed in electing a board member, because the ownership structure of most companies is so concentrated that the electoral quotient system does not work.[27]

In many countries, majority shareholders exercise significant influence over boards, directly as board members or indirectly through the appointment of board members who report to them. In this case, it is difficult to hold the ma-

---

26 In the event that neither the voting or non-voting minorities reach the required threshold separately, they may jointly elect one director with 10 percent of share capital.

27 Under the "electoral quotient" system, holders of voting shares cast their votes for competing lists of board members, each list making up the entire board, rather than for individual candidates. First, the total number of votes present at the annual general meeting is computed and the quotient Q is calculated by dividing this computed number by the total number of seats on the board up for election and rounding down Q to the lowest integer number. Second, holders of voting shares cast their votes for the competing lists of board members, and a tally is prepared. Each list, Ln, receives a number of votes, Vn. Third, the number of votes cast on each list is divided by the quotient Q. The result for a given list is a number consisting of an integer, In, and a fraction, Fn. Fourth, seats are allocated as follows. Each list of board members is first allocated as many seats on the board as its integer number. If the sum of the integer numbers is less than the total number of seats up for election or re-election, the remaining seat(s) are allocated on the basis of the highest fractions, in decreasing order.

jority shareholder liable for his actions as a "shadow director."[28] Malaysia has attempted to subject shadow directors to statutory duties.

The legal and regulatory frameworks in most assessed countries establish general duties for the board of directors. However, the prevailing legislation often does not spell out the key functions, and there are no guidelines or procedures on how to fulfill these obligations. In Mexico and Colombia, for example, director duties are not clearly specified in law and are left largely to bylaws. On the other hand, countries are beginning to introduce stiff penalties for board members who breach their duties without introducing the concept of the "business judgment rule." This rule allows directors to make business decisions without worrying about violating the duties of care and diligence, if they have acted on an informed basis, in good faith, and in the honest belief that the decision taken is in the best interests of the company. In the absence of such a rule, directors may be discouraged from taking necessary decisions in the ordinary course of business.

A common feature across all regions is the lack of training and the limited understanding that directors have of corporate governance issues. According to market surveys, nine out of ten directors do not feel that they are adequately informed or knowledgeable about their duties and responsibilities. A possible remedy is the creation of Institutes of Directors for training, dissemination of best practice and issuance of guidelines on board size, the constitution of committees, and other useful practices. Institutes of Directors have been created in a number of countries, including the Philippines, Brazil, and the Czech Republic. Training for directors is already mandatory in Malaysia.[29]

In addition to defining strategy, selecting, monitoring and overseeing management are other fundamental board functions. A board must be able to fire management. This requires a degree of independence from management (and controlling shareholders) that is generally lacking in developing countries and transition economies. In many countries with single tier board structures, the chief executive officer (CEO) also chairs the board. In developing countries where ownership is highly concentrated, this person often also represents the majority shareholders. This combination makes it virtually impossible for outsiders to replace management, since it would require management to fire itself. Therefore, the board fails in this fundamental respect. While it is tempting to

28 "Shadow directors" are controlling shareholders or shareholders with significant influence over the control of the company, who exert influence over the board even though they are not de facto directors.

29 Training is required for board members of banks in the Philippines.

recommend that the function of CEO be separated from that of board chair, experience in Morocco suggests that policymakers should carefully weigh the costs and benefits of such a recommendation. In Morocco, the business community supported the separation of CEO and chair, not because it would enhance the independence of the board from management, but because it diminished the chair's personal legal liability.[30] Hence if decoupling is to be a viable option, the accountability of board members to shareholders and stakeholders must first be firmly established. This may require changes to company law, or better enforcement of existing legislation. Another approach is to set up a special purpose committee empowered to select and monitor key management.

While there are non-executive directors on most boards in the countries surveyed, very few of them can be called truly "independent" from the controlling shareholder or management. The Kuala Lumpur Stock Exchange's listing requirements go beyond the norm by defining independent directors as "directors who are not officers of the company, who are neither related to its officers nor represent concentrated family holdings of its shares; who in the view of the company's board of directors, represent the interest of all public shareholders, and are free of any relationship that would interfere with the exercise of independent judgment."

Effective monitoring includes the detection and resolution of conflicts of interest between management/board and shareholders/stakeholders, and the prevention of any misuse of corporate assets and abuses in related party transactions. There is a growing consensus that board committees, such as nomination, remuneration, risk management and audit committees with independent directors, can be useful to assure independence from management in areas of potential conflict of interest. In almost all of the countries assessed, the board does not effectively ensure the integrity of accounting and financial reporting systems, including oversight over the audit function. At this stage, there is no consensus as to the optimal degree of independence.[31] In developing countries and transition economies, the pool of independent directors with financial and accounting knowledge is often limited. Mexico stands out among Latin American countries; 25 percent of directors in Mexican companies must be independent.

---

30 For this reason, a number of companies have opted for the two tier board structure.

31 Some, like the Australian Institute of Directors, argue in favor of director expertise over independence and that a majority of executive directors should be elected to key committees, like the audit committee. Others, like the American National Association of Corporate Directors, favor a majority of independent directors.

The OECD Principles state that board members must have access to accurate, relevant and timely information, including management accounts and outside advice. In most assessed countries with unitary boards, access to information is assured since most board members are insiders. However, information is not always readily available in countries with supervisory boards; likewise, independent directors often have trouble gaining access to information.[32]. Directors should also devote sufficient time to their responsibilities. In most countries surveyed, board meetings are still considered a formality and not convened with sufficient frequency.

Directors seldom prepare themselves adequately for board discussions, boards are often too large to be effective, and directors may not be limited as to how many board seats they may hold. One possible remedy is to introduce a listing rule requirement that companies publish information on the frequency and attendance of their board meetings in their annual report, as well as a limitation on the number of boards on which an individual may sit.

IV. Uses in Policy Dialogue and Implementation of Better Corporate Governance Practices

The corporate governance assessments are relevant to the countries surveyed, international financial institutions, policymakers and the private sector. They support diagnostic and strategic work, underpin policy dialogue and lending operations, and provide input to technical assistance and capacity building efforts. They are useful for companies who want to capture reputational benefits by improving their internal corporate governance structure.

1. Diagnosis, strategy and lending operations

The corporate governance assessments serve as building blocks for diagnostic work, such as investment climate assessments. They provide input into key policy documents, such as sectoral strategies for the private and financial sectors or countrywide development strategies. Their strengths lie in the systematic standardized coverage and in their benchmarking against an internationally recognized standard. The country-specific assessments complement the regional focus of the OECD/World Bank Roundtables on Corporate Governance. In addition to their diagnostic and strategic value, corporate governance country assessments help establish benchmarks for lending operations. In the

32 In India, for example, independent directors are often chosen with the tacit understanding that they will not actively exercise their right to company information.

World Bank, for example, the country program cycle has become the most important business model. Programmatic adjustment lending has been found to be a cost-effective vehicle for supporting the Bank's policy dialogue with clients on the social and structural agenda and for partnering with other agencies. The country has replaced the project as the critical focus of implementation. The Bank's programmatic approach has four main steps[33] – definition of the vision; diagnosis prepared and shared with clients and partners;[34] programming; and monitoring. Corporate governance country assessments help define the vision (the aspiration to comply with international standards). During the diagnostic phase, they provide critical, objective information on the strengths and weaknesses of an economy, including the functioning of the private sector and securities market. During the programming phase, the assessments play a role in the design and sequencing of operations. During the monitoring phase, they provide clear progress milestones to monitor program outcomes.

2. *Technical assistance and capacity building operations*

Corporate governance country assessments identify technical assistance and capacity building needs, which can be financed through operations from international financial institutions, bilaterals or the private sector. For example, the World Bank/OECD Global Corporate Governance Forum, a multi-donor trust fund, disseminates best practice, raises awareness of the need for reform, fosters academic research, and provides a source of finance for implementation of reform and capacity building.

Measures proposed in the assessments include: setting up institutes of directors; training securities regulators and commercial court magistrates; introducing arbitration procedures; strengthening associations of accountants and auditors; assisting with the drafting of a code of best practice (see Annex C); advising on the governance of the securities regulator and stock exchanges; training the financial press, and setting up shareholder advocacy institutions.

The corporate governance assessments can improve the focus of training by identifying areas where enforcement or capacity building need enhancement. Once training needs have been identified, the efficiency and targeting of delivery can be increased through an "output-based" approach to financing service delivery – allowing institutions to compete for the delivery of training –,

33 Source: *Tilmes, K./Velev, I./Gigler, K.*, "World Bank Documents: Programmatic Lending: Review of Recent Bank Documents," May 2001.

34 Due diligence and other diagnostic economic and sector work (ESW).

and linking trainer compensation to the number of students accredited in the skills.

A summary of follow up operations with a corporate governance dimension in client countries of the World Bank is set out in Annex E.

V. Open Issues and Next Steps

To enhance the relevance of the OECD Principles for developing countries and transition economies, the concept of choice and problems associated with enforcement must be debated.

1. Choice

A fundamental issue that arises from the corporate governance assessments is that choice, in the form of different corporate governance options for issuers, is an effective mechanism to facilitate reform. A "menu of options" approach provides a means for issuers and investors to choose the markets and companies most appropriate for their own risk profile. At the same time, standardization of options is desirable to lower transaction costs for issuers and investors.

All over the world, companies choose from among corporate forms with different obligations, the form best adapted to their needs. Choice of corporate form is therefore essential.

Choice is also desirable because it allows incentives to play their part. Issuers who want to attract portfolio investment have an incentive to adapt to norms that satisfy such investors. A stock exchange that allows listed firms to choose between different levels of disclosure and corporate governance standards through several listing segments, provides an opportunity for those companies choosing the segment with the highest standards to signal to investors that they are different from the majority of listed companies in their country. Such companies may be able to raise capital more easily, lower their cost of capital and attract high quality long-term investors, such as pension funds, as investors. This innovative approach provides a non-coercive mechanism for pulling the country's corporate governance upward gradually by leveraging reputational costs and benefits. Brazil's introduction of the *Novo Mercado* stock exchange compartment provides such an example. Companies listed on the *Novo Mercado* may not issue non-voting shares, must abide by U.S. GAAP or IAS, and their free float must be at least 25 percent. An arbitration panel has also been created to settle shareholder disputes.

At the other extreme, some companies may not be ready, willing or able to comply with the minimum disclosure, transparency and accountability standards of the OECD Principles, let alone those required by their exchange's "top segment"; however, they may still wish to provide some liquidity to shareholders. This aim can be achieved by introducing an Over-The-Counter (OTC) compartment, which provides limited disclosure standards but allows firms to offer shares through an organized market. This approach has been successful for the Czech Republic.

Investors have different risk profiles. Some are attracted by high-risk/high returns; some are more risk averse. Some may be willing to invest in a company with a limited degree of transparency, because they are confident in the management team or because they perceive the company's business sector to be especially lucrative. The co-existence of different corporate governance models provides a "horses for courses" approach, permits investors with different risk profiles to choose the market and company appropriate for them and allows market forces to pick the winners.

In addition, some developing nations with dynamic capital markets, like Chile, have liberalized their capital accounts, allowing pension funds to invest their savings abroad. While not necessarily appropriate for all developing countries and transition economies, one of the main benefits of this approach is that it provides alternative means of promoting equitable shareholder treatment, and creates strong incentives for issuers seeking capital and national regulators who want to promote overall economic fundamentals so that their financial systems comply with international standards.

2. *Enforcement*

In South and East Asia, Latin America and the Middle East/North Africa region, firms are often organized in business groups. These groups grow internally, constructing a web of companies that support the group. At the group's apex is a large family-controlled enterprise that fulfills a corporate finance function for smaller companies by financing suppliers and new firms and cushioning financial downturns. In Latin America and the Middle East, a bank or insurance firm is often added to the group, providing cross-holdings to finance growth. This system of internal corporate governance, while lacking transparency, substitutes for a weak external corporate governance framework, where the legislative framework is inadequate or legal enforcement is weak. Business groups function on the basis of proprietary information. Further discussion is required to determine whether rules and regulations concerning the dissemination of information and disclosure and transparency need to be adapted to these circumstances. Similarly, in countries with weak regulatory environments, concentrated enforcement through the market regulators may be preferable.

In developing countries and transition economies, where the legal and regulatory framework is evolving, the question arises whether policymakers should rely on judges or regulators to enforce laws and contracts. In countries with a well-functioning judicial system, private litigation may work well. In the countries assessed, however, courts are often under-financed, unmotivated, unclear as to how the law applies, unfamiliar with economic issues or even corrupt.[35] Experience shows that under these conditions, the incentives of regulators to enforce laws may be greater than those of judges. Judges are faced with a broader set of trade-offs and are less focused on corporate governance issues than securities regulators. It may be better to rely on regulatory agencies until the judicial system becomes efficient. This only works, however, if regulators can enforce sanctions without their verdicts being subject to automatic appeal. In Poland, strict enforcement of the securities law by a highly motivated regulator was associated with a rapidly developing stock market. In the Czech Republic, hands-off regulation and reliance on the court system was associated with a moribund stock market.[36]

3. *Other issues*

There are some areas where the OECD Principles remain open to discussion. The following topics are currently being debated in the context of the reassessment of the Principles.

Disclosure of compensation: The debate remains open on whether individual disclosure should be advocated in the Principles. Given that there is no consensus on this issue, flexibility is required to accommodate different rules and regulations. In Austria, aggregate disclosure is the norm. In Greece, the remuneration of the CEO must be disclosed, but not that of other executives. In the U.S., companies must disclose the remuneration of company directors, the CEO and the top four executives. This does not necessarily cover the top paid individuals. It has been pointed out that disclosure of individual remuneration drives compensation upward. The debate also remains open on whether stock options should be expensed in the company's P&L (Profit and Loss Statement).

---

35 *Glaeser, E./Johnson, S./Shleifer, A.*, "Coase versus the Coasians," *The Quarterly Journal of Economics*, Volume 116, Issue 3, pp. 853-899, 2001.

36 *Ibid.*

Beneficial ownership: The OECD Principles already require disclosure of major share ownership and voting rights, but at present remain silent on the issue of beneficial ownership. It is being argued by several quarters, that information on beneficial ownership and control rights is necessary for present and potential shareholders to assess their ability to influence the corporate governance process. It is also essential for identifying conflicts of interest, related party transactions and insider trading – transactions that are often to the detriment of minority shareholders. Finally, disclosure of beneficial ownership can also help prevent corruption, terrorist financing and money laundering. In France, for example, when beneficial ownership is not known, it is possible to strip the voting rights of the owner. IOSCO recommends that disclosure of substantial beneficial ownership be mandatory. The OECD has issued guidelines for the disclosure of beneficial ownership. Three options are set out in these guidelines, which may be cross-referenced in the Principles of Corporate Governance. However, several countries have also pointed out that anonymous ownership is legitimate. In addition, disclosure of beneficial ownership information requires some police powers. It has also been pointed out that allowing companies to have access to beneficial ownership information may be in contradiction with common law.

Disclosure of voting policies: There is a debate on whether institutional investors should be required to exercise their voting rights. Some quarters argue for disclosure of voting policy but stop short of mandating institutional investors to vote their shares. Greece, for example, has pointed out that disclosure of voting records will create costs.

Shareholders meetings: The notion that all shareholders resolutions should be binding on management is a concern in some countries. In the U.S. and Canada, for example, some resolutions are just advisory. The latter has pointed out that the company is responsible to the shareholders and the company. Responsibility to the company may require that some resolutions be just advisory.

Annex A: List of Standards and Codes Assessed by IMF and World Bank

Group A: Transparency Standards (assessed by the IMF, including under the FSAP)

- **Data Dissemination:** the Fund's Special Data Dissemination Standard/General Data Dissemination System (SDDS/GDDS).
- **Fiscal Transparency:** the Fund's Code of Good Practices on Fiscal Transparency.
- **Monetary and Financial Policy Transparency:** the Fund's *Code of Good Practices on Transparency in Monetary and Financial Policies* (usually assessed under the FSAP).

Group B: Regulatory and Supervisory Standards (assessed under the FSAP)

- **Banking Supervision:** Basel Committee's *Core Principles for Effective Banking Supervision* (BCP) (usually assessed under the FSAP).
- **Securities:** International Organization of Securities Commissions' (IOSCO) *Objectives and Principles for Securities Regulation.*
- **Insurance:** International Association of Insurance Supervisors' (IAIS) *Insurance Supervisory Principles.*
- **Payments Systems:** Committee on Payments and Settlements Systems' (CPSS) *Core Principles for Systemically Important Payments Systems.*

Group C: Market Infrastructure Standards (assessed by the World Bank, including under the FSAP)

- **Corporate Governance:** OECD Principles of Corporate Governance.
- **Accounting:** International Accounting Standards Committee's *International Accounting Standards.*
- **Auditing:** International Federation of Accountants' *International Standards on Auditing.*
- **Insolvency & Creditor Rights:** World Bank Principles and Guidelines for Effective Insolvency and Creditor Rights Systems.

Group D: Market Integrity Standards

Money Laundering: Financial Action Task Force (FATF) on Money Laundering *FATF 40 Recommendations* – preparation of ROSC modules under the aegis of the FATF currently under consideration.

Annex B: Chronology of the ROSC initiative

July 1998: IMF Executive Board indicates that the official sector should play a larger role in strengthening incentives to implement standards, including through monitoring the extent to which members observe standards in areas within the Fund's direct operational focus.

October 1998: G-22 Taskforce Recommendations – the G-22 working group recommends that the IMF, in the context of its Article IV surveillance consultations, should consider preparing a report ("Transparency Report"), which summarizes the degree to which an economy meets internationally recognized disclosure standards across a wide range of areas.

October 1998: G-7 endorses G-22 recommendation and calls on the IMF to "monitor in close co-operation with the standards-setting bodies the implementation of... codes and standards as part of its regular surveillance under Article IV."

1999/2000: IMF Executive Board decides to undertake reports on international financial architecture issues to be called "Transparency Reports." The World Bank joins the IMF in this exercise, which is expanded to include other assessments and subsequently called the "Reports on the Observance of Standards and Codes" (ROSCs).

Annex C: Codes of Best Practice

A code of best practice is a useful tool to complement the existing legal, regulatory and institutional framework underpinning corporate governance. Codes have been issued by companies seeking to differentiate themselves from their competitors in terms of corporate responsibility (General Motors, Royal Dutch Shell), by stock exchanges, and special purpose commissions set up by the private and the public sectors. A number of countries have issued national codes of best practice for corporate governance inspired by the OECD Principles. These include Brazil, India, Poland, the Czech Republic, Malaysia, Russia, and China, among others. While such codes are rooted in the OECD Principles, some of them go further. For example, India and South Africa require disclosure on individual emoluments of directors, including stock options – the OECD Principles do not. Likewise, in Brazil, the *Novo Mercado* requires issuers to adhere to the one-share-one-vote principle – the OECD Principles do not.

Codes of best practice are rules that go beyond the law. They are an instrument for improving behavior based on evolving best practice. They consist of guidelines concerning the selection, composition, and remuneration of the board of directors, the role and composition of board committees, the definition of "independence," the treatment of shareholders and stakeholders, accounting standards, financial and non financial reporting and disclosure policies. Compliance with the code is usually voluntary. In Malaysia and Singapore, the securities regulator and/or stock exchange require issuers to disclose the extent to which they comply with the code in their annual report and explain divergences, or to publish a separate report on corporate governance. In countries such as India and Brazil, some of the recommendations of the code have been picked up by the securities regulator or the stock exchange and made mandatory through the listing requirements (e.g. minimum number of independent directors).

Annex D: ROSC Summary Matrix

The matrix below shows the scoring for the 20 ROSCs that have been approved by country authorities for publication on the World Bank's ROSC website at http://www.worldbank.org/ifa/rosc_cg.html as of September 2003. A summary assessment without scores has been approved and published for Hong Kong. In cases where more than one ROSC was carried out (i.e. the Czech Republic), only scores for the latest assessment are included. Assessments carried out in 2000 had three scores: "Yes," "No," and "Incomplete." The next generation of assessments, conducted through December 2001, had four scores: "Observed," "Largely Observed," "Materially Not Observed" and "Not Observed." In January 2002, the score of "Partially Observed" was introduced. Section "II.B. Process and Format" of the contains a detailed explanation of the scores. The first generation of assessments did not cover stakeholder rights and some other minor issues, as indicated by the entry "Not available." For assessments published prior to March 2002, the OECD sub-Principles were scored; subsequently, only the main Principles have been scored.

OECD PRINCIPLES	AFRICA (SUB-SAHARAN)			EAST ASIA AND PACIFIC		EUROPE AND CENTRAL ASIA									LATIN AMERICA AND CARIBBEAN			MIDDLE EAST AND N. AFRICA		SOUTH ASIA
	South Africa	Mauritius	Zimbabwe[3]	Malaysia[3]	Phillipines[1,2]	Bulgaria	Croatia[1,2]	Czech[2]	Georgia	Hungary	Latvia	Lithuania	Poland[3]	Turkey[3]	Chile	Colombia	Mexico	Egypt[1,2]	Morocco[1,2]	India[3]
Section I: The Rights of Shareholders																				
A. Basic shareholders rights	O	PO				LO		LO		PO	LO	LO			LO	LO	LO			
(i) Ownership registration			Y	Y	LO		LO		LO				Y	I				LO	LO	I
(ii) Share transfer			Y	Y	O		MNO		LO				Y	I				O	MNO	I
(iii) Access to information			Y	Y	MNO		LO		MNO				I	Y				LO	LO	I
(iv) Participation and voting at AGM			Y	Y	O		LO		MNO				Y	Y				LO	LO	Y
(v) Election of board			Y	Y	O		LO		MNO				Y	Y				LO	LO	Y
(vi) Share in the profit			Y	Y	O		LO		MNO				Y	Y				O	O	Y

OECD PRINCIPLES	AFRICA (SUB-SAHARAN)			EAST ASIA AND PACIFIC		EUROPE AND CENTRAL ASIA									LATIN AMERICA AND CARIBBEAN			MIDDLE EAST AND N. AFRICA		SOUTH ASIA
	South Africa	Mauritius	Zimbabwe[3]	Malaysia[3]	Phillipines[1,2]	Bulgaria	Croatia[1,2]	Czech[2]	Georgia	Hungary	Latvia	Lithuania	Poland[3]	Turkey[3]	Chile	Colombia	Mexico	Egypt[1,2]	Morocco[1,2]	India[3]
B. The right to participate in decisions on fundamental corporate changes	LO	PO				MNO		PO		O	LO	LO			O	PO	PO			
(i) Amendments to the statutes			Y	Y	O		LO		MNO				Y	Y				O	O	Y
(ii) Authorization of additional shares			Y	Y	O		MNO		MNO				N	Y				O	LO	Y
(iii) Extraordinary transactions (resulting in sale of the company)			Y	Y	LO		MNO		MNO				I	Y				O	LO	Y
C. The right to be adequately informed about, participate and vote in general shareholder meetings (AGM)	PO	PO				LO		PO		LO	LO	O			LO	PO	PO			
(i) Sufficient and timely information about AGM			Y	Y	LO		O		MNO				Y	Y				O	LO	Y
(ii) Opportunity to ask question and place items on agenda			NA	NA	NO		MNO		LO				Y	Y				LO	LO	NA
(iii) Vote in person or in absentia			Y	I	O		LO		MNO				I	I				LO	LO	I

OECD PRINCIPLES	AFRICA (SUB-SAHARAN)			EAST ASIA AND PACIFIC		EUROPE AND CENTRAL ASIA									LATIN AMERICA AND CARIBBEAN			MIDDLE EAST AND N. AFRICA		SOUTH ASIA
	South Africa	Mauritius	Zimbabwe[3]	Malaysia[3]	Phillipines[1,2]	Bulgaria	Croatia[1,2]	Czech[2]	Georgia	Hungary	Latvia	Lithuania	Poland[3]	Turkey[3]	Chile	Colombia	Mexico	Egypt[1,2]	Morocco[1,2]	India[3]
D. Disclosure of capital structures and arrangements enabling control disproportionate to equity ownership	O	PO	N	I	O	PO	LO	PO	MNO	LO	MNO	MNO	Y	Y	PO	MNO	PO	LO	MNO	I
E. Efficient and transparent functioning of market for corporate control	LO	PO				LO		O		LO	LO	MNO			LO	MNO	LO			
(i) Clearly articulated and disclosed rules and procedures, transparent prices and fair conditions			N	Y	LO		LO		MNO				N	I				LO	MNO	Y
(ii) No use of anti-takeover devices to shield management from accountability			NA	NA	NO		LO		MNO				NA	NA				O	MNO	NA
F. Requirement to weigh costs/benefits of exercising voting rights	NO	NO	NA	NA	NO	NO	MNO	NO	NO	PO	MNO	MNO	N	NA	LO	NO	NO	NO	NO	NA

OECD PRINCIPLES	AFRICA (SUB-SAHARAN)			EAST ASIA AND PACIFIC		EUROPE AND CENTRAL ASIA									LATIN AMERICA AND CARIBBEAN			MIDDLE EAST AND N. AFRICA		SOUTH ASIA
	South Africa	Mauritius	Zimbabwe[3]	Malaysia[3]	Phillipines[1,2]	Bulgaria	Croatia[1,2]	Czech[2]	Georgia	Hungary	Latvia	Lithuania	Poland[3]	Turkey[3]	Chile	Colombia	Mexico	Egypt[1,2]	Morocco[1,2]	India[3]
Section II: Equitable Treatment of Shareholders																				
A. Equal treatment of shareholders within same class	PO	PO				LO		PO		NO	PO	LO			LO	PO	PO			
(i) Same voting rights for shareholders within each class. Ability to obtain information about voting rights attached to all classes before share acquisition. Changes in voting rights subject to shareholder vote.			Y	Y	LO		LO		MNO				Y	Y				O	O	Y
(ii) Vote by custodians or nominees in agreement with beneficial owner.			NA	NA	O		NO		MNO				NA	Y				LO	NO	NA
(iii) AGM processes and procedures allow for equitable treatment. Avoidance of undue difficulties and expenses in relation to voting.			Y	Y	O		MNO		MNO				Y	Y				O	LO	I

OECD PRINCIPLES	AFRICA (SUB-SAHARAN)			EAST ASIA AND PACIFIC		EUROPE AND CENTRAL ASIA									LATIN AMERICA AND CARIBBEAN			MIDDLE EAST AND N. AFRICA		SOUTH ASIA
	South Africa	Mauritius	Zimbabwe[3]	Malaysia[3]	Phillipines[1,2]	Bulgaria	Croatia[1,2]	Czech[2]	Georgia	Hungary	Latvia	Lithuania	Poland[3]	Turkey[3]	Chile	Colombia	Mexico	Egypt[1,2]	Morocco[1,2]	India[3]
B. Prohibition of insider-trading and self-dealing	O	PO	N	Y	LO	LO	LO	MNO	MNO	O	LO	LO	Y	Y	PO	MNO	LO	LO	MNO	Y
C. Disclosure by directors and managers of material interests in transactions or matters affecting the company	PO	PO	I	Y	MNO	NO	LO	MNO	MNO	LO	LO	LO	Y	I	LO	NO	PO	LO	MNO	I
Section III: Role of Stakeholders in Corporate Governance																				
A. Respect of legal stakeholder rights	O	PO	NA	NA	LO	PO	LO	MNO	LO	LO	LO	LO	NA	NA	LO	O	LO	O	MNO	NA
B. Redress for violation of rights	O	PO	NA	NA	MNO	PO	MNO	PO	MNO	LO	LO	LO	NA	NA	PO	PO	LO	O	MNO	NA
C. Performance-enhancing mechanisms for stakeholder participation	LO	MNO	NA	NA	MNO	PO	MNO	PO	LO	LO	LO	O	NA	NA	LO	LO	LO	O	MNO	NA
D. Access to relevant information	O	LO	NA	NA	MNO	LO	MNO	LO	LO	LO	PO	MNO	NA	NA	O	O	O	LO	LO	NA

OECD PRINCIPLES	AFRICA (SUB-SAHARAN)			EAST ASIA AND PACIFIC		EUROPE AND CENTRAL ASIA									LATIN AMERICA AND CARIBBEAN			MIDDLE EAST AND N. AFRICA		SOUTH ASIA
	South Africa	Mauritius	Zimbabwe[3]	Malaysia[3]	Phillipines[1,2]	Bulgaria	Croatia[1,2]	Czech[3]	Georgia	Hungary	Latvia	Lithuania	Poland[3]	Turkey[3]	Chile	Colombia	Mexico	Egypt[1,2]	Morocco[1,2]	India[3]
Section IV: Disclosure and Transparency																				
A. Disclosure of material information	PO	PO				PO		PO		LO	PO	PO			PO	PO	LO			
(i) Financial and operating results			Y	Y	O		MNO		MNO				Y	Y				LO	MNO	Y
(ii) Company objectives			NA	NA	O		MNO		MNO				I	NA				LO	MNO	NA
(iii) Major share ownership and voting rights			N	Y	O		MNO		MNO				Y	Y				MNO	MNO	Y
(iv) Board members, key executives and their remuneration			I	NA	LO		MNO		MNO				I	I				LO	LO	I
(v) Material foreseeable risk factors			NA	NA	LO		MNO		MNO				N	I				MNO	NO	N
(vi) Material issues regarding employees and other stakeholders			NA	NA	NO		MNO		MNO				NA	I				LO	NO	NA
(vii) Governance structures and policies			N	N	NO		MNO		NO				N	NA				MNO	NO	N

OECD PRINCIPLES	AFRICA (SUB-SAHARAN)			EAST ASIA AND PACIFIC		EUROPE AND CENTRAL ASIA									LATIN AMERICA AND CARIBBEAN			MIDDLE EAST AND N. AFRICA		SOUTH ASIA
	South Africa	Mauritius	Zimbabwe[3]	Malaysia[3]	Phillipines[1,2]	Bulgaria	Croatia[1,2]	Czech[2]	Georgia	Hungary	Latvia	Lithuania	Poland[3]	Turkey[3]	Chile	Colombia	Mexico	Egypt[1,2]	Morocco[1,2]	India[3]
B. Preparation of information, audit, and disclosure in accordance with high standards of accounting, disclosure, and audit	PO	LO	Y	I	MNO	PO	MNO	MNO	MNO	LO	PO	MNO	I	I	PO	MNO	PO	LO	MNO	I
C. Annual audit by independent auditor	PO	PO	Y	I	MNO	PO	MNO	LO	LO	PO	PO	MNO	I	Y	PO	MNO	PO	LO	O	I
D. Channels for disseminating information allow for fair, timely, and cost-efficient access to information by users	LO	LO	NA	Y	MNO	PO	MNO	LO	MNO	O	LO	LO	Y	Y	LO	O	O	LO	LO	Y
Section V: Responsibilities of the Board																				
A. Act on an informed basis, in good faith, with due diligence and care, in the best interest of the company and shareholders	PO	PO	Y	I	MNO	MNO	LO	PO	LO	PO	PO	LO	I	Y	PO	PO	PO	LO	LO	Y
B. Fair treatment of each class of shareholders	LO	PO	Y	I	LO	MNO	LO	PO	MNO	PO	PO	LO	Y	Y	PO	MNO	PO	LO	O	Y
C. Compliance with law and taking into account stakeholders' interests	O	PO	NA	NA	LO	MNO	LO	PO	LO	PO	O	LO	NA	Y	LO	LO	LO	O	LO	NA

OECD PRINCIPLES	AFRICA (SUB-SAHARAN)			EAST ASIA AND PACIFIC		EUROPE AND CENTRAL ASIA									LATIN AMERICA AND CARIBBEAN			MIDDLE EAST AND N. AFRICA		SOUTH ASIA
	South Africa	Mauritius	Zimbabwe[3]	Malaysia[3]	Phillipines[1,2]	Bulgaria	Croatia[1,2]	Czech[2]	Georgia	Hungary	Latvia	Lithuania	Poland[3]	Turkey[3]	Chile	Colombia	Mexico	Egypt[1,2]	Morocco[1,2]	India[3]
D. Key functions	PO	PO				MNO		PO		LO	PO	LO			PO	MNO	PO			
(i) Corporate strategy, risk policy, budgets, business plans, performance objectives, implementation and performance surveillance, major capital expenditures, acquisitions, divestitures			I	I	MNO		MNO		MNO				I	I				LO	LO	I
(ii) Selection, monitoring, replacement of key management			Y	I	MNO		MNO		LO				Y	Y				LO	LO	I
(iii) Key executive and board remuneration, board nomination			I	I	MNO		MNO		LO				NA	Y				LO	LO	I
(iv) Monitoring of conflict of interest of management, board members, and shareholders, including misuse of corporate assets and abuse in related party transactions.			NA	I	MNO		MNO		NO				I	I				MNO	MNO	I

OECD PRINCIPLES	AFRICA (SUB-SAHARAN)			EAST ASIA AND PACIFIC		EUROPE AND CENTRAL ASIA									LATIN AMERICA AND CARIBBEAN			MIDDLE EAST AND N. AFRICA		SOUTH ASIA
	South Africa	Mauritius	Zimbabwe[3]	Malaysia[3]	Phillipines[1,2]	Bulgaria	Croatia[1,2]	Czech[2]	Georgia	Hungary	Latvia	Lithuania	Poland[3]	Turkey[3]	Chile	Colombia	Mexico	Egypt[1,2]	Morocco[1,2]	India[3]
(v) Ensuring integrity of accounting and financial reporting systems, including independent audit, systems of control, compliance with law			Y	Y	MNO		MNO		NO				I	I				LO	LO	I
(vi) Monitoring governance practices and making necessary changes			NA	NA	NO		MNO		NO				NA	Y				MNO	NO	NA
(vii) Overseeing disclosure and communication			Y	Y	LO		MNO		NO				NA	Y				LO	NO	Y
E. Objective judgement on corporate affairs	PO	MNO				MNO		PO		PO	LO	LO			PO	MNO	PO			
(i) Assignment of non-executive board members to tasks of potential conflict of interest (e.g. financial reporting, remuneration)			N	I	NO		MNO		LO				NA	I				MNO	LO	N
(ii) Devote sufficient time to their responsibilities			NA	NA	MNO		MNO		MNO				NA	Y				LO	MNO	N
F. Access to accurate, relevant, and timely information	LO	PO	NA	NA	MNO	MNO	MNO	LO	NO	LO	LO	LO	NA	Y	LO	O	O	O	LO	NA

Annex E: Summary of Follow-Up Operations in Select Countries/Regions, as of September 2003	
Brazil	$808m PAL (01-02) to support CG reform; TA of $14.5m (01) to enhance financial transparency, regulation of capital markets.
Bulgaria	$150m PAL pending (Feb 03) for CG legislative reform.
Colombia	$150m PAL (Apr 03) focuses on financial markets reform.
Czech Republic	CG assessment of insurance sector conducted Apr 03.
Egypt	$247 IDF grant (Jan 02) to set up Institute of Directors.
Korea	CG reform elements in SAL I & II; $300,00 ASEM grant, $750,000 PHRD Special to develop CPE program; WB support to improve Financial Supervisory Service's effectiveness, professional training; Korean IOD established.
Latvia	TA on financial institution governance provided to central bank.
Lithuania	CFAA prepared in 2002.
Mauritius	Accounting and Auditing ROSC completed FY03.
Morocco	Dissemination of key findings conducted Jun 03.
Philippines	TA to support director training, sector specific issues handled under SILS, APLS. $21.9m judicial reform support project initiated, CG foundation established with private sector support.
Romania	CG provisions proposed to be included as part of PAL I.
Turkey	Corporate governance included in draft AAA report on Non-Bank Financial Institutions.
Ukraine	PAL (02-03) includes shareholder rights provisions.
Europe and Central Asia Region	$40,000 ECA KIF grant to support regional Institute of Directors.

ACRONYMS:

AAA: Analytical and Advisory Activities
APL: Adaptable Program Lending
ASEM: Asian Financial Crisis Response Trust Fund
CFAA: Country Financial Accountability Assessment
CG: Corporate governance
KIF: Knowledge Innovation Fund
PAL: Programmatic Adjustment Loan
PHRD: Policy and Human Resources Development Fund
CPE: Continuing Professional Education
IDF: Institutional Development Fund
SAL: Structural Adjustment Loan
SIL: Specific Investment Loan
TA: Technical assistance

EL-SHAGI EL-SHAGI

IS GLOBALISATION DETRIMENTAL FOR DEVELOPING COUNTRIES?

The globalisation of world economy has vastly expanded since the beginning of the 1990s. This manifests itself not only in the strong increase of the flow of trade and the greater increase in capital transactions, but above all in the huge expansion of the flow of information. The latter is due to the rapid progress of information and communication technology.[1]

Critics of globalisation bemoan that globalisation has brought on numerous negative consequences for developing countries.[2]

My remarks will illustrate that these fears are unfounded. It could be maintained that globalisation actually brings relatively more advantages to developing countries than to developed countries. As far as international trade relations are actually harming developing countries, this harm is not a result of opening up to the global economy but rather of interventions and restrictive foreign trade measures that the industrial nations and developing countries place upon themselves.

I. The Perceived Disadvantages Brought on by Globalisation

In the context of complaints regarding the negative effects of globalisation for developing counties the primary arguments specified are:[3]

---

1 Cf. i.a. *El-Shagi, M./Schröder, J.*, Die Neue Ökonomie und ihre Bedeutung für die internationale Arbeitsteilung, in: *Reitz, S.*: Theoretische und wirtschaftspolitische Aspekte der internationalen Integration, Festschrift für Helga Luckenbach zum 68. Geburtstag, Berlin 2003, p. 51-65; and *Filc, W.*, Internationale Finanzbeziehungen, Trier 2002.

2 For a general discussion of the arguments produced by the critics of globalisation, particularly from the industrialized nations' perspective, cf. *Donges, J. B./Freytag, A.*, Allgemeine Wirtschaftspolitik, Stuttgart 2001, p. 262 ff; *May, B.*, Widerstand gegen die Globalisierung. Sind die Befürchtungen der Globalisierungsgegner gerechtfertigt? in: Internationale Politik, No. 7, vol. 56, p. 27-34; and *Peterson, H.-G.*, Globalisierung und soziale Gerechtigkeit, in: *Reitz, S.*, ibid., p. 187-221.

3 Cf. i.a. the numerous statements of Attac in the internet and ist publications (http://www.attac-netzwerk.de and the links given on that page); Deutscher Bundestag: Schlussbericht der Enquete–Kommission Globalisierung der Weltwirtschaft – Herausforderungen und Antworten. Drucksache 14/9200, Berlin 2002; and *Stiglitz, J. E.*, Globalization and its Discontents, London u. a. 2002.

- The pressure of competition caused by the qualitatively superior offers from industrial nations will displace production in the developing countries and thereby impair the development of productive capacity in the developing countries.
- Developing countries will be at a disadvantage as they receive unfair and insufficient payment for their exports while the active work force in the export sector receives a lower wage compared to the work force in industrial nations, leading to a "disproportionate exchange".
- The pressure of international competition and the advent of competition between developing countries in the course of globalisation will impede or even entirely prevent an improvement of the employees' social situation in developing countries, since price wars leave little room for the funding of social welfare. In this context the trend and the need for cheaper production is responsible for the employment of child workers.
- Globalisation is held responsible for the increase of environmental problems. This accusation is raised not only in the context of the general increase in worldwide pollution caused by emissions due to forced economic growth and the increasing rise in transport activities. Critics of globalisation suggest that globalisation causes particular environmental damage in developing countries. The particularly large increase in pollution in these counties is traced back primarily to the catch-up process, the relaxed environmental policies in developing countries and the reallocation of environmentally damaging investments into the countries in question.
- Last but not least, globalisation is deemed to increase the instability of developing countries and newly industrializing nations that have become intertwined with the world economy. In this context, critics refer to situations such as the Asia Crisis in South East Asia, which occurred in the second half of the 1990s, and the various crises that occurred in Latin American countries during the last ten years such as Brazil, Mexico and Argentina.

II. Untenability of these Arguments

1. The fear of replacement of national industries

The belief that the replacement of national industries is a negative outcome of globalisation is untenable. The division of work whether within or between national economies inevitably and naturally coincides with the decline in production in some sectors of the national economy and expansion in others. As long as prices are not distorted by state intervention or other measures, this process takes place in accordance with comparative advantages. Therefore, whoever perceives as a problem the replacement of some national industries due to integration in the world economy, must consequently be in favour of sacrificing the division of work respectively and the use of comparative advantages, which would be incomprehensible. The replacement of national production in free trade represents a problem only in certain cases where particular distortions are present. In essence, this holds true for the following scenarios:

- When, in terms of Friedrich List, so called "infant industry problems" prevent young industries to use their potential comparative advantages effectively, temporary "protection" may be necessary to enable these industries to achieve competitive maturity.
- When the social costs of production and respectively the opportunity costs of the products which are displaced through import are lower than their private costs and consequently lower than the relevant import prices, due to wages exceeding the opportunity costs of labour and insufficient remuneration flexibility; or
- If the costs of the products competing with or which are replaced by imports compared to the costs of export production reflects a significant disadvantage to the products competing with imported products; this may be the case where export production passes on part of its costs to society as technological externalities, such as for example the disutility through environmental pollution caused by production.

None of these circumstances, however, justify protection against the world economy.[4]

- With regard to the "infant-industry-argument" it should be taken into account that it is virtually impossible, to identify in advance those industries which, under the shield of temporary protection, will develop to reach competitive maturity and will be able to face international competition. This is illustrated by the fact that in many developing countries, industries have been protected over a long period of time without ever succeeding to become competitive. Furthermore, it should be noted, that

---

4 Cf. *El-Shagi, E.-S.*, Plädoyer für die Liberalisierung des Welthandels, in: List Forum für Wirtschafts- und Finanzpolitik, vol. 19 (1993), p. 183-206; and *id.*, Handelsgewinne, Handelsrestriktionen und Annahmen der Außenhandelstheorie, in: Zeitschrift für Wirtschaftspolitik, vol. 37, p. 251-263.

opening up towards the world economy brings about various integration benefits (both static and dynamical) to developing countries, which contribute significantly to development in these countries (for example through the improvements of possibilities to import capital goods and to finance the improvement of the infra structure) thereby encouraging the development of competitive industries without favouring protection.

- Too high or inflexible wages can hardly justify the protection of developing countries from foreign competitors. Wages higher than the opportunity costs of labour, in the case where they occur in sectors competing with imports in developing countries, are generally a result of state intervention such as inadequate wage policies. In this case, protection policies are merely attempting to cure the symptoms whilst bypassing the real causes. It can be assumed that, in the absence of state intrusion, inflexibility of wages occurs less frequently in developing countries than in industrialized nations, since labour unions in developing countries generally have less power and social safeguards against redundancy are predominantly insufficient. Moreover, the disposition to accept wage cuts in industries competing with imports is favoured by the often-high unemployment rates and often diminutive wages in alternative activities.
- And potential high non-internalised environmental costs produced by export production justify neither protection for competing import products nor export restrictions for the concerned export products. In such a case, it would in fact be advisable to encourage the internalisation of the concerned external effects by according environmental policies.

2. *The accusation of unfair prices and unjust wages due to "disproportionate exchange"*

The accusation of unfair prices is misleading: Why should free market prices be "unfair"? As long as the purchaser is not forced to trade with a specific supplier or vice versa, both the purchaser and supplier will benefit from the concerned transaction – provided they act rationally. To suppose that purchasers from the industrial nations have a greater power in the market and due to this can receive a larger cut in the profits, is not an argument against globalisation but rather one in favour of it. Globalisation strengthens competition – also among the purchasers from industrial nations – and thereby may benefit even the weaker suppliers in developing countries. Likewise, the accusation regarding "disproportionate exchange" in terms that workers in developing countries receive a lower wage for comparable work, which is seen as exploitation, does not stand firm on an objective practical inspection. Differences and discrepancies in wage between workers in developing countries and industrial nations are justifiable by a range of different factors which in no way represent any disadvantage to these countries, such as the fact that

- workforces in developing countries are generally less scarce than in industrial nations,
- they are generally less qualified,
- correspondingly, production is greatly labour intensive, which works towards the reduction of marginal productivity of labour,
- the profitability of investments in these developing countries is often affected by infrastructural deficits and a higher risk potential posed by unsatisfactory basic conditions, and finally
- reliance on foreign selling markets often raises the costs and thereby reduces the opportunity to pay higher wages.

3. The accusation of negative social effects

The charge that globalisation has negative social effects due to the pressure on prices which impairs the funding of social welfare institutions is equally insupportable. The intensification of foreign economic relations and transactions increases the national product and thereby increases the state's own abilities to finance and improve social welfare. The fact that some countries are trying to prevent pressure on labour costs by attempting to avoid increases in social insurance contributions should not be condemned as unsocial, since a reduction in the expansion of labour costs generally allows for a growth in employment. Correspondingly, a restrictive policy concerning the increase of social insurance contributions is more social in the end.[5]

Likewise the criticism of globalisation in social terms, referring to the occurrence of child labour in some export industries in developing countries, is not convincing. In these circumstances we need to consider what the children concerned would do and what their standard of living would be like if their income derived from the export sector were to fall away.

4. The accusation of increasing environmental pollution

Undoubtedly, unregulated environmental pollution, i.e. pollution not modulated by taxes and measures providing for internalisation of additional social

5 Cf. *El-Shagi, E.-S.*, "Soziale Marktwirtschaft" – wohlgemeinte Idee mit negativen Folgen für die marktwirtschaftliche Ordnung, in: List Forum für Wirtschafts- und Finanzpolitik, vol. 23 (1997), No. 4, p. 348-362.

costs (and technological externalities respectively), will result in allocation distortions and welfare forfeits. This holds true for environmental damage occurring inside a specific country as well as for international and global pollution. The allegation that the globalisation of the world's economy inevitably strengthens such allocation distortions and losses in welfare, and even brings on further disadvantages for developing countries, is questionable. The increase in transport activities in the course of globalisation through the intensification of international trade may in fact constitute a possible source of additional environmental pollution. However, this will only result in the growth of allocation distortions and welfare losses if pollution through transport activities is not accompanied by adequate internalisation measures. Provided that environmental costs are internalised, increased transport activities caused by the intensification of trade will generally be accompanied by an additional increase in net welfare.

The assumption that developing countries in particular suffer losses due to the environmental consequences effects of globalisation is not evident anyway, since a correct evaluation of environmental damage according to the individual preferences of developing countries would as a rule result in a lower assessment of environmental loss.[6] This is supported firstly by the low level of income in the developing countries and secondly by the fact that (up to now) there has been a lower level of environmental pollution in the countries in question. Consequently, these countries perceive additional burdens on the environmental media in the course of globalisation as a minor impairment of social welfare compared to the realised globalisation advantages. It is in the interest of these countries, to attract environmentally intensive investments as long as the necessary internalisation orientated environmental policies are put into action, because after the adjustment of environmental costs the said direct investments result in positive contributions to growth and employment.

5. The risk of greater instability

The higher instability in the course of globalisation is above all explained by the intensiveness of capital transactions.[7] Thus, the outbreak of the Asian cri-

---

6 Cf. *El-Shagi, E.-S.*, Umweltpolitik als grenzüberschreitende bzw. globale Aufgabe, in: WiSt, 1/2004, p. 14-19.

7 Cf. i.a. *Donges, J. B.*, Globale Finanzmärkte, Währungskrisen und aufstrebende Volkswirtschaften, in: Zeitschrift für Wirtschaftspolitik, vol. 48 (1999), No. 2, p. 129-146; und Sachverständigenrat zur Begutachtung der gesamtwirtschaftlichen Entwicklung: Jahresgutachten 1998/99. Deutscher Bundestag, Drucksache 14/73, especially p. 214 et seq.

sis in 1997, for example, was the result of concentrated and massive capital export after a longer period of capital inflow. In 1997, the five countries which were hit hardest (Thailand, Indonesia, Korea, Malaysia and the Philippines) had to cope with a private net capital drain of about 12 billion US dollars after they had obtained a private capital inflow of 93 billion US dollars in 1996. This turn in capital movement did not only lead to the collapse of currency exchange rates, but also brought about a significant slump in prices on the stock market. Likewise, the real estate markets suffered – after a period of overheating – severe price incursions. These incursions in both capital and property markets due to the withdrawal of foreign capital were aggravated by sales by nationals.

The outlined problems expanded to the economy as a whole, leading to the insolvency of business companies and banks. Particularly those companies, which had raised credit abroad experienced difficulties due to the fall of national currency exchange rates; banks were afflicted by the increase in bad credits and its level of debt in US dollar.

In a globalised world economy with freedom of capital movement, such regional crises can hardly be prevented but the probability of their occurrence as well as their intensity can be reduced. Primarily, this should be attainable through the improvement of market conditions that ensure the proper functioning of the market both within the individual national economies and in the global economy. The more or less abrupt cumulative withdrawal of capital which triggers such crises is, as a rule, the consequence of previous wrong management decisions and disappointed investor expectations. The reduction of the information deficit and asymmetries through the disclosure of information that allows for a better estimation of the economic situation, the expected developments in the target countries and a better analysis of the target countries and companies' risks, would probably reduce the danger of wrong decisions concerning capital flow. At the same time it must be taken into account that, to a considerable extent, the failings and errors of economic policy in the countries concerned are responsible for the crises. In the context of the Asia crisis, it should be noted that:[8]

- the countries concerned have formally or informally bound their currency exchange rates to that of the USD. Following the upward revaluation of the dollar in 1996/97, this had an adverse effect upon their competitiveness and a negative effect on their trade balance and finally led to a loss

8 Cf. *El-Shagi, E.-S.*, Die Asienkrise: Ausmaß, Ursachen, Folgen, in: Orientierungen zu Wirtschafts- und Gesellschaftspolitik, 77 (3/1998), p. 2-5.

of confidence especially regarding foreign investor contributions. The attempts by these countries to uphold the exchange rates of their currencies against the US Dollar lead to an increase of interest rates compared to the US Dollar area and most other industrial nations. This induced an increase in raising credit abroad, in particular US Dollar credit, whereby hedging of exchange rates risks was generally neglected. In Thailand for example banks took up US dollar credits to allow credits to domestic companies at a higher interest rate.

- Generally, deficiencies of the East Asian banking system aided and abetted in the breakout of their own crisis by pursuing an expansive credit policy that did not take account of security needs adequately. The supervision of commercial banks was insufficient, the behaviour of provisions regulating banks inadequate and the transparency of business methods and economic results deficient.

The endeavours of the concerned East Asian countries to overcome these deficiencies with the assistance of the IMF (International Monetary Fund) and to improve the basic conditions for competition attained considerable success. Approximately three years after the outbreak, some of these countries already showed signs of recovery that countries in the EU could only dream of.

It is also important to state that these crises most frequently hit countries that had obtained significant positive results due to their advanced integration in the world economy and had reached a level of development, not far below that of most industrialized nations. This suggests that problems arising in the course of globalisation cannot be solved by restricting or even abandoning the world economy, but rather by improving the functional requirements in the markets just as no one would seriously advise to relinquish cars and an excellent road network to prevent car accidents.

III. Distribution of Globalisation Profits

It is not only the fears regarding disadvantages to developing countries through globalisation and world economic integration that are untenable. A closer examination illustrates that developing countries and new industrial nations have in relative terms profited more from worldwide integration than the old highly developed industrials countries.

The use of comparative advantages and the advantages of complementary trade is likely to result in a greater effect on prices and relatively larger profits for developing countries and smaller economies in general than for larger and industrialized nations. The greater effect on prices results from the fact that the opening up to the global economy leads to a relatively higher rise of demand for products for which developing countries possess comparative advantages respectively for which they have a supply advantage, than for the products for which the production and supply advantages lie on the side of developed countries; as a consequence, the prices of these products rise higher than the export prices of large national economies. In the area of import, at the same time, small and developing countries benefit from the relatively larger expansion of supply of import products compared to developed economies by trade with developing countries – at least where substitutive trade is concerned.

Through massive global expansion, intensification and the cut in costs within the information sector due to the development in information and communication technology, developing countries will be able to obtain integration profits on a relatively larger scale than developed countries. This is due to the fact that in developing countries, inadequate information about foreign markets impair the absorption of integration advantages more significantly than in industrialized nations. A further advantage of this technology is that as it is new industrial nations do not have a head start due to their long experience, as is the case in industrial production. Correspondingly, highly developed industrial nations of today like Germany attempt to draw IT specialists from developing countries like India.

Likewise, it can be observed that, regarding the international movement of capital, developing countries and especially the advanced nations among them, as well as the newly industrialised, nations attract foreign direct investment to an increasing degree. This applies all the more, the more qualified and semi-skilled workers are available, and the better the infrastructural situation and general conditions for entrepreneurial activities are. Compared to industrialised countries, developing countries benefit relatively more from a number of integration advantages, particularly dynamic integration profits – resulting from the opening up of markets in developing countries, vis-à-vis the established industrial nation:

- It is obvious, for example, that the transfer of technology, whether through trade or direct investment, generally occurs from the advanced countries to the developing ones.
- Furthermore, it is hardly conceivable that underdevelopment could be overcome without the import of goods needed for investment from the industrial nations, which means overcoming low accessibility of technology in developing countries.
- Likewise, the use of unemployed resources through the expansion of demand as a result of external trade (*vent vor surplus*) will be of greater im-

portance to developing countries. This is not only due to the fact that the expansion of demand is relatively stronger for developing countries compared to the developed countries; the factor proportions also peak for this mobilising effect in developing countries. Developing countries dispose of a relatively larger workforce compared to industrialised countries. Correspondingly, they are generally vested with comparative advantages in the area of labour intensive production. The increase in demand for these products results in an increased demand for workers, and where unemployed workers are available, this leads to a rise in employment, rather than an increase in wages.

- Moreover, an improved utilization of economies of scale may play a major role for developing countries because these countries generally have tighter national markets. The orientation of sale to these markets alone, inevitably degrades the possibilities for the use of economies of scale in production.
- Finally, the intensification of competition through foreign trade is more important for developing countries, since the narrowness of the market in many of these countries makes monopolisation and the domination of the market easier.

IV. Conclusion

The claim that the opening up of developing countries towards the world economy coinciding with an increase in globalisation tendencies in these countries is detrimental for them is unsustainable. In fact the opposite is true. Developing countries profit significantly from integration into the global economy. This integration is a fundamental basis for their sustainable development. They depend more strongly on integration of the global economy than the industrial nations and profit relatively more from this integration compared to the latter.

Disadvantages for developing countries in the area of foreign trade relations hardly arise from liberalisation and the opening up of these countries to the world economy. Rather, they arise from questionable interventions and restrictive practices of the industrial nations towards these developing countries and from the restrictive practices and questionable interventions that developing countries place upon themselves. On the side of the industrial nations, the massive competitive distortions resulting from agricultural policy need to be pointed out and the fact that foreign trade restrictions of industrial nations against developing countries are generally more pronounced than the restrictions on other industrial nations also need to be mentioned. It is particularly problematic that the restrictions are stronger in areas where the developing countries hold comparative advantages industries such as the textile, clothing and steel industries.

To understand the problem of restrictive politics from the point of view of developing countries, it is sufficient to compare the massive development performances of countries that have placed more emphasis on market economies and integration into the world economy, like the East Asian Tiger nations, with the failure of those countries which have over a long period of time impeded their own development by socialist experiments, like many Arab states.[9]

---

9 Cf. *El-Shagi, E.-S.*, Die Überlegenheit des marktwirtschaftlichen Entwicklungswegs, in: "Argumente der Freiheit", edited by *Friedrich-Naumann-Stiftung*, Sankt Augustin 1992; and *Langhammer, R. J.*, Das Soziale in der Globalisierung: Zwischen Gutgemeintem und Gutem, in: Volkswirtschaftliche Korrespondenz der Adolf-Weber-Stiftung, No. 2/02, vol. 41, München 2002.

DISCUSSION

Professor Dr. Roland *Eckert* (Trier) started the discussion by expressing his doubts about Professor Dr. El-Shagi *El-Shagi's* (Trier) view that corporate governance could be successful without state legislation or international contracts. Looking back on his 30 years of lecturing, he recalled discussions with Marxist students and colleagues. Being very convinced of the functioning of their system, they had attributed failures not to the system, but to the conditions under which the system had had to work. Methodologically this was an efficient way to immunize a theoretical concept. Now he recognized that same method on the side of liberalism where he had once come from. Failures were attributed not to the deficiency of market mechanisms, but to the deficiency of external factors like the state, the banking system etc. In *Eckert*'s view, one main problem NGOs such as "attac" were confronted with is the fact that there is a world economy, but not a world state. In fact, they did not fight globalisation; they pointed their fingers at a globalisation process driven only by economic forces. They sought state guaranteed rules for the economy. *Eckert* pointed out that the present process of globalisation empowered multinational corporations to an extent that they had become a lot more powerful than individual states – citing the oil companies in Nigeria as an example. Under the interpretation suggested by *El-Shagi*, problems like these were not addressed, because the dominant theory explaining globalisation was immunized against failures within its theoretical construct.

Then Professor Dr. Paul *Buteux* (Winnipeg) criticized the widespread use of the expression "globalisation", in his opinion a portmanteau word. He interpreted *El-Shagi*'s understanding of the word globalisation with respect to developing countries as being full participants in a global market economy. Despite their general agreement, he considered himself a neo-classicist in contrast to *El-Shagi*. However, the conditions of a true global market economy do not exist at present. Instead, there was a set of regional and overlapping economies: This had to do with the structure of many developing countries and the very strong interest groups in developed countries, visible at the collapsed WTO conference in Cancun. Another example was the protection of dying industries such as the North American and European steel industries.

He found that, nowadays, we had a dominant political ideology of so called "liberalism". The best though controversial manifesto of that was Francis Fukuyama's "Idea of the end of history". In this manifesto market economy is regarded as being the dominant ideology.

Referring to the frequently used term "public goods", *Buteux* said that he understood public goods to be provided for the benefit of those providing them. Others may benefit as well. If good corporate governance did in fact constitute a public good, it still remained open who was going to provide it and who was going to benefit.

Professor Dr. Peter *Eigen* (Berlin) praised the speech on corporate governance by Mr. Olivier *Frémond* (Washington) and stressed that the very clear and precise definition of corporate governance *Frémond* had given in his speech should be recognized in the discussion on global governance. Corporate governance was a very small, but important part of global governance, designed to protect the interests of shareholders. He considered it a weakness of the report that it was based on the time prior to the Enron collapse, based on the "arrogance" of the American corporate sector that everyone had to live up to their standards in order to become a full member of the global economy. In this report, 18 countries had been reviewed, not including the U.S.. He was extremely interested to see the revision of this report in Paris this fall.

Eigen supported *El-Shagi*'s view that globalisation was taking place and that it would make no sense to oppose it, even though it was imperfect in its reach. However, he tried to challenge *El-Shagi*'s laissez-faire approach. In his view, it did not represent the current leading opinion. There was a change within the world bank to create institutions for intervention in the economic development. The problem, he stated, was that effective and selective intervention of state institutions was not working on a global basis. Therefore, global governance appeared like a Swiss cheese, whose holes could not be filled by seeking answers from the market anymore. This was supported by the IMF, the World Bank, and scholars of international relations. Institutions would have to be strengthened to protect the functioning of the market, the environment and other aspects of global governance.

El-Shagi made clear that he was neither neoclassic nor did he support a laissez-faire position. He saw himself close to *Friedrich Hayek* and the old liberal school, which describes even neoclassicism as static and a step back for economics. Moreover, *Hayek* had stated that laissez-faire was the biggest mistake of liberalism ever. Liberals worked towards a functioning competition. in which the national government had several responsibilities. The first task of the state was to create the basis for a functioning competition – i.e. to provide for the safety of the person and private property, protection of competition and the distribution of public goods, since the market mechanism was not able to do this because of the character of the public good. He repeated that market mechanisms did not solve all problems, giving environmental protection as an example. Furthermore, the comparison of Marxism with Liberalism was totally wrong. This could not only be proven historically the optimisation of command economy was also only a theoretical system far from reality – e.g. involving knowledge of private preferences.

Frémond distinguished three distinctive characters of norms: They could either be public, private or semi-public. He qualified codes of good practice as semi-public laws. He stated that in corporate governance the UK approach was increasingly adopted: under this "comply or be disclosed" approach, non-compliance with a rule leads to a disclosure which works when issues of reputation are at stake.

Frémond then remarked that in a lot of transition countries, there was need for enforcement if the law was not to be a mere piece of paper. Speaking of the legal framework in many transition economies the issue of coherence must be dealt with. Many of these countries imported legislation in one field from different legal systems. Giving the example of Czech corporate law he argued that sometimes they were not very good matches.

On the term "public good", *Frémond* clarified that the externalities created by the behaviour of certain countries have an influence on other states. As an example he referred to the financial crises in Asia suddenly affected Latin America, Russia and shook the whole world. Therefore, he concluded, there was a need to create a world standard to prevent and mitigate crises.

Concerning the question of benefits from corporate governance the speaker named portfolio investors and equity investors. Furthermore he emphasized that looking at the flows of capital, there had been a dramatic shift in the proportion of private flows and public flows: public flows had once been very significant compared to private flows, today it was the other way around. Private flows consisting of foreign direct investments and portfolio investments had become essential, because developing countries – not having enough internal resources – need external capital to fund their growth. Therefore the World Bank is strengthening the possibilities for foreign portfolio investors to invest in developing countries by enhancing corporate governance. It is equity investors and of course all other stakeholders in a corporation such as employees who benefit. In his eyes corporate governance deals with "residual claimants", i.e. those investors who had taken the residual risk. This risk could not be predicted, so they should have financial claim on the allocation of profits. All other stakeholders are protected by specific contracts. *Frémond* concluded that none of the 28 countries assessed on their respect of OECD principles of corporate governance had fully complied.

Frémond explained that he sees corporate governance as one little stone in the pyramid of measures that need to be put in place in order to strengthen the international architecture and prevent the occurrence of financial crises. There is a need for investors' confidence by to entrust their savings to capital markets.

Professor Dr. Matthias *Ruffert* (Jena) asked *Frémond* on the issue of legitimacy. He understands the concept of corporate governance with its aspect of benchmarking as a modern way of standard setting. But these rules are not made by an international treaty, which then has to be ratified by national parliaments. He asked if the World Bank was aware of the constitutional problems this implies. He gave the example of the German Corporate Governance Codex which is not a statute but a codex to which enterprises and economic actors can adhere to or not. Rules are imposed without parliamentary backing: "The hole in the Swiss cheese here is democratic legitimacy". Secondly, he asked whether there was a change in World Bank policy regarding the issue of democracy or if it still treated this as being part of so called "*domaine reservé*" of states.

Frémond declared that the approach of the World Bank was to promote choice as much as possible. He regards choice as an engine of change and reform. He would prefer this in place of trying to adopt a more legalistic cohesive attitude towards corporate governance. He also argued that there should be a certain extent of non-binding rules for corporations that let the market regulate itself. He is convinced that there is no desire to codify these principles of corporate governance into a piece of legislation. Rather he would like to see compliance through a fear of reputation loss for corporations.

Concerning the question whether democracy was an objective of the World Bank, *Frémond* pointed out that the World Bank supports democracy and – not knowing if it is an official policy of the World Bank – he made it clear that there are some conditions before a market economy can function efficiently which are freedom of speech and freedom of association. In developing countries, he admitted, the western model did not work, because there was a need for concentrated ownership structure and a need for somebody who substantially controls the block of ownership to align the interests.

BERND VON HOFFMANN*

CONCLUSIONS

I. Prohibition of Force in International Law

According to international law, the monopoly for the exertion of military force as set out in Art. 51 of the UN Charter lies exclusively with the Security Council of the United Nations, except in the case of self defence or assent of the state in question. In the absence of such justification, the exertion of military force by the member states of the UN constitutes a breach of international law. The prohibition of force in international law cannot be invalidated by numerous violations by the member states nor by unilateral revocation of this obligation.

II. Weakness of Enforcement Structures

Undeniably, the prohibition of force has been violated by various states, without the result of sanctions under international law. At the same time, the factual possibilities to enforce decisions of the Security Council are insufficient. Particularly the lack of permanent troop access has proved to be detrimental to the Council's authority.

The weakness of the sanctions available under international law should not result in the return to the exertion of military force by individual states. In fact, it is necessary to render the enforcement mechanisms of the Security Council more effective. To achieve this, the UN member states need to ensure an effective supply of UN troops by providing the Security Council with sufficient military forces. Several options are available to realise this goal. At present, it seems unrealistic, however, to demand the conclusion of separate treaties as set out in Art. 43 of the UN Charter, which would provide the Security Council with access to its own military force. The other option which is practised frequently is the deployment of troops under a mandate authorized by the Se-

* These conclusions have been drafted on the basis of a brainstorming conducted after the last session of the workshop in collaboration with Professor Dr. Christine *Langenfeld*, Göttingen, Professor Dr. Paul *Buteux*, Manitoba, Professor Dr. Roland *Eckert*, Professor Dr. El-Shagi *El-Shagi*, Professor Dr. Bernd *von Hoffmann* and Professor Dr. Meinhard *Schröder*, Trier, and Dr. Wolfgang *Weiß*, Bayreuth, identifying the most important issues of discussion which had been touched upon in the course of the workshop.

curity Council which are provided by UN member states or by an international military alliance such as NATO. It is contrary to the duties of UN member states to refuse participation in the enforcement of Security Council decisions in advance and at the same time condemn states that resort to individual action.

III. Reform of the United Nations

Although a fundamental reform of the UN's constitution may be desirable in the long term, it is neither realistic nor urgently required at present. Instead, small steps of improvement are necessary, which can be realized without amending the UN Charter. The efficiency of the Security Council's enforcement procedures, for example, could be increased without changing the rules of the Charter. Likewise, the Global Compact Initiative of the UN Secretary General demonstrates that global governance initiatives do not presuppose the introduction of new competences to the UN Security Council.

IV. Common Values?

In western countries, certain common values, particularly human rights, are deemed to have global validity. A number of states, however, do not fully adhere to these western standards or perceive these values to be of less fundamental importance according to their own traditional value system.

Hence, the question whether and to what extent a consensus on common values at a global or a regional level exists, remains unsettled. Its clarification is urgently required, since it is *inter alia* essential to the determination of commonly accepted standards for the admissibility and preconditions as well as the limits of humanitarian intervention.

V. The Role of the European Union

Due to its cultural and economic standing, the European Union ought to be a main actor of a multi-polar world order. So far, its role has been characterised by dissent on fundamental issues, especially on the question of exerting military force. If the member states of the European Union could succeed in reaching a common standpoint on questions of global governance, and creating effective enforcement mechanisms Europe could develop into a global player with a potential equivalent to that of the United States of America. Discontent with the current unilateral leading position of the United States of America should result in the creation of the institutional preconditions necessary to put the full potential of the European Union into practice.

VI. Actors

For incalculable time, nation states will remain the main actors of the world order. The basic conditions of a global framework are still determined by the nation states. As a consequence of this dominance of nation states, global welfare needs remain rather neglected in the face of the nation states' shared interest to preserve their power. Therefore, the consideration and implementation of necessary provisions at a global level requires a set of actors that focuses on global welfare. These actors encompass international organizations as well as non-governmental organizations (NGOs). International business is increasingly realigning its activities to the global economy as a whole. Despite the fact that the focus of international business is not primarily concerned with global welfare, its interest may well correspond to those of actors engaged in the advancement of global welfare. This is visible, for example, in the combat against corruption, in which the World Bank and NGOs such as Transparency International (TI) or the ICC take part in a coordinated action.

VII. Process

Alongside the classic instruments of the international legal order (international treaties, international organizations), novel instruments appear. The implementation of world standards of corporate governance in developing countries provides a good example: The standards referred to are laid down in the guidelines of the OECD. The World Bank recommends that member states adopt these standards and implement them into national law. Upon request by implementing states, the World Bank reviews the implementation of the standards and issues a certificate, which is recognized worldwide.

The uncoordinated coexistence of international organizations pursuing parallel objectives frequently results in useless duplication of effort and dissonant valuation. So far, no mechanisms for the coordination of activities of these diverse organizations have been developed. No transparent determination of policies exists. This lack of coordination is illustrated by the divergences of the development policies of World Bank and WTO.

VIII. Developing Countries

In the long term, free market economy ensures the best development results for both developing countries and industrialized nations. Protectionism prevents adjustment to an efficient international division of labour and impairs dynamic development. Hence, the demand to open the markets and to withdraw restrictions imposed on foreign trade is not only directed to developing countries, but also and with equal emphasis to the western developed countries. Their demand for developing countries to open their markets for industrial products and services remains unpersuasive as long as they themselves refuse to open their own markets to agricultural products and services from third world countries.

The transition from protectionism to open markets involves problems of adjustment. The consequences for social welfare need to be cushioned by transitional provisions and flanking socio-political measures. The development results expected from a free market economy can be achieved only within a regulatory framework that guarantees free competition and ensures the protection of common welfare interests such as environmental protection and social welfare.

LIST OF PARTICIPANTS

Prof. Dr. *Paul Buteux,* Professor of Political Studies, University of Manitoba and Director of the Centre for Defence and Security Studies, University of Manitoba; member of the Board of Directors of the Atlantic Council of Canada, and the Canadian Institute of Strategic Studies.

Prof. Dr. *Klaus Dicke,* speaker, Professor at the University of Jena, Chair of "Political Theory and History of Ideas"; member of the German United Nations Association, the German Society for Political Science, the German Society of International Law and of the Scientific Advisory Council on Issues of the United Nations at the Foreign Office.

Prof. Dr. *Roland Eckert,* Professor of Sociology at the University of Trier; member of the advisory councils "Bündnis für Demokratie und Toleranz" of the German Government, of the committee preparing the First Security Report of the German Government and of the Institute for Interdisciplinary Research on Conflict and Violence of the University of Bielefeld.

Prof. Dr. *Peter Eigen*, speaker, former World Bank manager of programs in Africa and Latin America; founder and chairman of Transparency International (TI); member of the Advisory Council of the Center for International Development at the John F. Kennedy School of Government and of the UN Global Compact Advisory Commission; Professor h.c. of Political Science at Freie University of Berlin.

Prof. Dr. *El-Shagi El-Shagi,* speaker, Professor of Economics at the University of Trier, Chair of International and Development Economics.

Olivier Frémond, speaker, Program Coordinator of the Corporate Governance Unit of the Private Sector Development Department at the World Bank.

Prof. *Michael J. Glennon,* speaker, Professor of International Law at the Fletcher School of Law and Diplomacy, Tufts University, in Medford, Massachusetts; in 2000 Consultant to U.S. Department of State (use of force); member of the American Law Institute and the Council on Foreign Relations.

Prof. Dr. *Bernd von Hoffmann,* Professor of Civil, Comparative and Private International Law in Trier; 1992 Lectures Hague Academy of International Law Board, Board Institute of Legal Policy, Trier.

Prof. Dr. *Christine Langenfeld,* Professor of Public Law at the University of Göttingen.

Prof. Dr. *Hanns W. Maull,* speaker, Chair for Foreign Policy and International Relations at the University of Trier; member of the Center for Asia Pacific Studies of the University of Trier.

Prof. Dr. *Stefan Oeter,* Professor for Public Law, European Community Law and Public International Law at the University of Hamburg Law School and managing director of the Institute of International Affairs of the University of Hamburg.

Angelika Pohlenz, speaker, Secretary General, International Chamber of Commerce (ICC) Germany, Cologne; member of the small and medium-sized business Committee of DIHK, the Foreign Trade Committee of DIHK and of the Foreign Trade Committee of BDI.

Prof. Dr. *Gerhard Robbers,* Professor for Public Law at the University of Trier; director of the Institute for European Constitutional Law and director of the Institute for Legal Policy, judge at the Administrative Court of Appeals Rhineland-Palatine.

Prof. Dr. *Matthias Ruffert*, Professor of Constitutional and Administrative Law with European Law at the Friedrich-Schiller-Universität Jena.

Prof. Dr. *Meinhard Schröder,* speaker, Professor of Law for Domestic and Foreign Public Law, Public International Law and European Law at the University of Trier; judge at the Regional Court of Appeal Rhineland-Palatine; co-founder and director of the Trier Research Institute on Environmental and Technical Law (IUTR).

Prof. Dr. Dr. h.c. *Daniel Thürer,* LL.M., Professor of International, European, Public and Comparative Constitutional Law, University of Zurich; Founding Director of the "Europa Institut an der Universität Zürich".

Dr. *Wolfgang Weiß*, speaker, Assistant Professor of Public Law, European and Public International Law at University of Bayreuth, Germany; in winter semester 2003/4 Guest Professor of Public International Law at University of Munich, Germany.

Rechtspolitisches Symposium
Legal Policy Symposium

Herausgegeben im Institut für Rechtspolitik an der Universität Trier
von Bernd von Hoffmann und Gerhard Robbers

Band 1 Bernd von Hoffmann (ed.): Towards a Common European Immigration Policy. Reports and Discussions of a Symposium held in Trier on October 24th and 25th, 2002. 2003.

Band 2 Bernd von Hoffmann (ed.): Global Governance. Reports and Discussions of a Symposium held in Trier on October 9th and 10th, 2003. 2004.

www.peterlang.de